The COMPANIONS in Christ™ Network

www.companionsinchrist.org

So much more!

Companions in Christ offers leaders *so much more* than just printed resources. It offers an ongoing LEADERSHIP NETWORK that provides:

- Opportunities to connect with other churches who are also journeying through *Companions in Christ*
- Helpful leadership tips and articles as well as updated lists of supplemental resources
- Training opportunities that develop and deepen the leadership skills used in formational groups
- A staff available to consult with you to meet the needs of your small group
- An online discussion room where you can share or gather information
- Insights and testimonies from other *Companions in Christ* leaders
- A FREE 48-page *Getting Started Guide* filled with practical tools to help you start a group in your church
- FREE *Companions in Christ* posters to use as you promote the group in your congregation

Just complete this card and drop it in the mail, and you can enjoy the many benefits available to leaders through the *Companions in Christ* NETWORK!

- ❑ Add my name to the *Companions in Christ* NETWORK __mailing list__ so that I can receive ongoing information about small-group resources and leadership trainings.
- ❑ Add my name to the *Companions in Christ* NETWORK __email list__ so that I can receive ongoing information about small-group resources and leadership trainings.
- ❑ Please send me a FREE 48-page *Getting Started Guide.*
- ❑ Please send me FREE *Companions in Christ* posters. Indicate quantity needed: _____

Name: _____

Address: _____   _____

City/State/Zip: _____

Church: _____

Email:_____ Ph_

D1305760

WOFLG

For information about dates and locations of *Companions in Christ*
Leader Orientations (Basic One-Day Training) and
Leader Trainings (Advance Three-Day Training) visit

www.companionsinchrist.org

Fold here and tape

Please include your return address:

_____

_____

_____

BUSINESS REPLY MAIL
FIRST-CLASS MAIL PERMIT NO. 1540 NASHVILLE TN

POSTAGE WILL BE PAID BY ADDRESSEE

COMPANIONS in Christ

UPPER ROOM MINISTRIES
PO BOX 340012
NASHVILLE, TN 37203-9540

COMPANIONS
in Christ

The Way of Forgiveness

A Small-Group Experience
in Spiritual Formation

LEADER'S GUIDE

Stephen D. Bryant and Marjorie J. Thompson

UPPER ROOM BOOKS
NASHVILLE

Cover design: Bruce Gore
Design and implementation: Lori Putnam
Cover art: Carter Bock
Cover art rendering: Marjorie J.Thompson
First printing: 2002

Library of Congress Cataloging-in-Publication

Bryant, Stephen D.
Companions in Christ: the way of forgiveness leader's guide/
Stephen D. Bryant and Marjorie J. Thompson
      p. cm.
    Includes bibliographical references.
    ISBN 0-8358-0981-1
    1. Forgiveness—Religious aspects—Christianity. 2. Forgiveness—Study and teaching. 3. Church group work. I. Thompson, Marjorie J., 1953– II. Title.
BV4647.F55 .B79 2002
253' .7—dc21   2002005427

Printed in the United States of America

For more information on *Companions in Christ*
call 1-800-972-0433 or visit www.companionsinchrist.org

Contents

Weekly Needs at a Glance

*P*rior to your first *Way of Forgiveness* meeting, review this Weekly Needs at a Glance list to familiarize yourself with what is needed at the Preparatory Meeting as well as each of the eight weekly meetings. Knowing required items well in advance will help you avoid last-minute crises. As you can see, all items but one are readily available. The one exception is the Peace, Hope, and Justice prayer candle introduced in Week 4. The Leader's Guide includes simple instructions for creating a similar candle. However, after reading the explanation of the candle below, you may decide to purchase one of the originals on behalf of your group.

Explanation of the Peace, Hope, and Justice Prayer Candle

The Peace, Hope, and Justice prayer candle celebrates the truth that the light of Christ shines through the darkness, pain, and violence in the world, symbolized by the barbed wire that surrounds the candle. Individuals and groups are invited to light the candle daily (or regularly), while at the same time taking a moment to pray for a particular situation of struggle and pain in the world.

The original prayer candle served as an important symbol of resistance against apartheid in South Africa. It was lit during services of worship while the names of those in government detention were read aloud and prayed for. To this day the prayer candle remains a powerful symbol of protest against injustice and suffering in the world.

This particular candle is handcrafted by unemployed people living in Ivory Park, an impoverished informal settlement area in South Africa near Johannesburg where Upper

Room Ministries has an outreach center. For most of the craftspeople, this is their only source of income. All net proceeds from the sale of this candle benefit those craftspeople through the Nehemiah Project, an economic empowerment project created by two Methodist churches in South Africa. Note that the craftsperson who made your candle has signed it on the bottom.

By purchasing this candle, you and your group are already lighting a candle in the midst of darkness in one corner of the world.

Hobson United Methodist Church offers these candles in support of South Africa. To order, make a $20.00 contribution payable to "Hobson UMC." Mailing address is Hobson UMC, c/o Janet Wolf, 1512 Cedar Lane, Nashville, TN 37212 (USA).

Weekly Materials

PREPARATORY MEETING

- Christ candle (any large white candle) and cloth for worship table
- Extra Bibles
- Hymnals/songbooks
- Extra copies of *The Way of Forgiveness* Participant's Book and *Journal* if you think some members may need them
- Flip chart and marker; write group ground rules on flip chart in advance (page 20)
- "Talking piece" (page 30)
- A list of other *Way of Forgiveness* Groups (per instructions on page 27)
- Card titled "Prayer for Our *Companions in Christ* Group" (from the back of this Leader's Guide)

WEEK 1   LIVING IN GOD'S BLESSING

- Christ candle and cloth for worship table
- Extra Bibles
- Hymnals/songbook
- Robe (red if possible)
- Ring
- Sandals

- Rembrandt painting reproduction (cut from the back of your Participant's Book)
- Newsprint with group litany response written out

WEEK 2   RELEASING SHAME AND GUILT
- Christ candle and cloth for worship table
- Extra Bibles
- Hymnals/songbooks
- A stone for each participant and a container in which to carry these
- A strip of cloth 2–3 feet long and 1 inch wide for each participant
- A copy of "Meditation with John 11" for each participant from pages 46–47 of the Leader's Guide

WEEK 3   FACING OUR ANGER
- Christ candle and cloth for worship table
- Extra Bibles
- Hymnals/songbooks
- Colored markers or crayons

WEEK 4   TRANSFORMING ANGER
- Christ candle and cloth for worship table
- Extra Bibles
- Hymnals/songbooks
- Peace, Hope and Justice prayer candle
- One small votive or tea candle for each group member
- A copy of the "Reflection Sheet on Transforming Anger" for each participant from page 59 of the Leader's Guide

WEEK 5   RECEIVING GOD'S FORGIVENESS
- Christ candle and cloth for worship table
- Extra Bibles
- Hymnals/songbooks
- Table large enough to seat all the members of your group
- Cups and a beverage

- Napkins, plates, cheese, fruit, and bread (utensils if needed)
- Piece of bread for each participant (perhaps a quarter piece of pita bread)
- Peace, Hope, and Justice prayer candle
- A bulletin board or designated place to display the stories of forgiveness participants are collecting weekly

WEEK 6   FORGIVING OTHERS

- Christ candle and cloth for worship table
- Extra Bibles
- Hymnals/songbooks
- Copies for each person of the "Reflection Sheet on Your Debtor's Prison" from page 74 of the Leader's Guide
- Large pottery or glass bowl filled with water and ½ inch of sand in the bottom
- Container filled with small, smooth stones ("River rocks" can be purchased by the bag at Pier 1 Imports.)
- Peace, Hope, and Justice prayer candle
- A bulletin board or designated place to display the stories of forgiveness participants are collecting weekly

WEEK 7   SEEKING RECONCILIATION

- Christ candle and cloth for worship table
- Extra Bibles
- Hymnals/songbooks
- Magazines, newspapers, and scissors
- Bowl of water and container of stones (from previous meeting)
- Peace, Hope, and Justice prayer candle
- A bulletin board or designated place to display the stories of forgiveness participants are collecting
- Pictures of the September 11, 2001, attack on the World Trade Center

WEEK 8   BECOMING THE BELOVED COMMUNITY

- Christ candle and cloth for worship table
- Extra Bibles
- Hymnals/songbooks
- Small bowl
- Oil
- Small crosses for each participant
- Peace, Hope, and Justice prayer candle
- A bulletin board or designated place to display the stories of forgiveness participants are collecting

Acknowledgments

The original twenty-eight-week *Companions in Christ* resource grew from the seeds of a vision long held by Stephen Bryant, editor/publisher of Upper Room Ministries, and given shape by Marjorie Thompson, director of the Pathways Center of Upper Room Ministries.The vision, which has now grown into the *Companions in Christ* series, was realized through the efforts of many people over many years. It is important, then, that we acknowledge not just those individuals who were instrumental in the development of *Companions in Christ: The Way of Forgiveness*, but that we also express gratitude to those who envisioned and contributed to the foundational work, *Companions in Christ*.

Companions in Christ: The Way of Forgiveness

Companions in Christ: The Way of Forgiveness is the second title in a series of small-group resources that began with the original *Companions in Christ*. The progression for the eight-week journey and the writing of the weekly articles in the Participant's Book for *Companions in Christ: The Way of Forgiveness* are the primary work of Marjorie Thompson. The daily exercises and the Leader's Guide are the shared work of Marjorie Thompson and Stephen Bryant in consultation with a staff advisory group that included Lynne Deming, Cindy Helms, and Tony Peterson. An additional group made important contributions to *The Way of Forgiveness*, especially to the daily exercises in the Participant's Book and the "Deeper Explorations" in the Leader's Guide. This group was comprised of individuals who were experienced in spiritual formation or who took part in the development of the original resource, *Companions in Christ*. They provided valuable insight and theological guidance as well. This group included John Anderson, W. G. Henry, Wynn McGregor, John Penn, Flora Slosson Wuellner, and Carole Cotton Winn.

Companions in Christ

The core resource, *Companions in Christ*, was the result of a team of persons who shared a vision for creatively engaging persons in a journey of spiritual growth and discovery. The work of these people laid the foundation for each book in the *Companions in Christ* series. Janice T. Grana served as editor. The authors of the chapter articles were Gerrit Scott Dawson, Adele Gonzalez, E. Glenn Hinson, Rueben P. Job, Marjorie J. Thompson, and Wendy M. Wright. Stephen Bryant was the primary author of the daily exercises and the Leader's Guide. Marjorie Thompson created the original design and participated in the editing. Keith Beasley-Topliffe served as a consultant in the creation of the process for the small-group meetings and contributed numerous ideas that influenced the final shape of the resource. Members of advisory groups were Jeannette Bakke, Avery Brooke, Thomas Parker, Helen Pearson Smith, Luther E. Smith Jr., Eradio Valverde Jr., Diane Luton Blum, Carol Bumbalough, Ruth Torri, and Mark Wilson. Prior to publication of the resource, the following churches participated as test groups:

First United Methodist Church, Hartselle, Alabama
St. George's Episcopal Church, Nashville, Tennessee
Northwest Presbyterian Church, Atlanta, Georgia
Garfield Memorial United Methodist Church, Pepper Pike, Ohio
First United Methodist Church, Corpus Christi, Texas
Malibu United Methodist Church, Malibu, California
First United Methodist Church, Santa Monica, California
St. Paul United Methodist Church, San Antonio, Texas
Trinity Presbyterian Church, Arvada, Colorado
First United Methodist Church, Franklin, Tennessee
La Trinidad United Methodist Church, San Antonio, Texas
Aldersgate United Methodist Church, Slidell, Louisiana

Introduction

Welcome to *Companions in Christ: The Way of Forgiveness*, a small-group resource designed to help your small group explore Christ's call to live a forgiven and forgiving life. Over the course of eight weeks, we will explore the movement from shame, guilt, and anger to forgiveness and reconciliation. The larger context for this exploration is Jesus' understanding of the blessed life, expressed in his teachings from the Sermon on the Mount (Matthew 5–7). These teachings comprise some of the most profound and spiritually challenging ideas we could ever hope to realize in our lives. It is a privilege to struggle with the challenge. Perhaps like Jacob wrestling with the angel (Gen. 32:22-32), we will emerge from the struggle with a blessing if we ask for it!

This resource is the second title in the Companions in Christ series that began with the twenty-eight week original resource in spiritual formation called simply *Companions in Christ*. Each title of Companions that follows the original program is intended to further expand on the core content using the same basic format. In the foundational resource, *Companions in Christ*, we explored the Christian spiritual life under five headings: Journey, Scripture, Prayer, Call, and Spiritual Guidance. Each subsequent title of the Companions in Christ series will explore in greater depth some aspect of one of these primary categories of spiritual practice.

The Way of Forgiveness falls under the heading of Christian vocation or call. Forgiveness and reconciliation are practices that give concrete expression to our calling as disciples of Jesus. They say something extremely profound about the way we are called to live out our faith in the world of daily realities, few of which are ideal. Not many persons would claim it is an easy matter to learn to forgive those who have wounded us or to be reconciled to our enemies. The demands of Christian discipleship are challenging, to say the least. Jesus asks of us nothing short of complete conversion of life—a transformation of mind, heart, and action that reveals ever more fully the beauty and wholeness of his own life and spirit in us. This is what it means to be conformed to the image of Christ, the goal of spiritual formation in the Christian tradition. It is a daunting challenge, one that we cannot consider apart from the grace of God. Yet we can claim a theological heritage that affirms that such grace has already been made available to us in the person of Jesus Christ and is continually available to us through the gift of the Holy Spirit. We gain access to grace most readily through prayer, faith, love for the deep truths and promises of scripture, a willingness to be guided by the Spirit, and by offering our best talents in God's service.

So we invite you now to open yourself inwardly to the grace that may be given during this exploration of your call in Christ to forgive and be reconciled. Claim boldly from God whatever you feel you need to approach this topic. Perhaps no practices can bring us closer to the mind and heart of Christ than these blessed attitudes and actions.

About the Resource and Process

Like all resources in the Companions in Christ series, *The Way of Forgiveness* has two primary components: (1) individual reading and daily exercises throughout the week with the Participant's Book and (2) a weekly two-hour meeting based on suggestions in the Leader's Guide. The Participant's Book has a weekly reading that introduces new material and five daily exercises to help participants reflect on their lives in light of the content of the reading. These exercises help participants move from information (knowledge *about*) to experience (knowledge *of*). An important part of this process is keeping a personal notebook or journal where participants record reflections, prayers, and questions for later review and for reference at the weekly group meeting. The daily exercise commitment is about thirty minutes. The weekly meeting will include time for reflecting on the exercises of the past week, for moving deeper into learnings from the weekly readings, for having group experiences of prayer, and for considering ways to share with the congregation what has been learned or experienced.

The material in *Companions in Christ: The Way of Forgiveness* covers a period of nine weeks, a preparatory meeting followed by eight weeks of content that moves through each of the following areas:

1. *Living in God's Blessing*: Receiving our blessed identity in God with gratitude and living in the fullness of that blessing.

2. *Releasing Shame and Guilt*: Recognizing shame and guilt in our lives, and how they separate us from the blessing of God.

3. *Facing Our Anger*: Identifying types of anger and assessing the impact they have on us and others.

4. *Transforming Anger*: Exploring practices to transform anger into constructive energy.

5. *Receiving God's Forgiveness*: Opening to a more complete understanding of forgiveness and a willingness to receive it.

6. *Forgiving Others*: Moving toward a desire and capacity to forgive those who wound us.

7. *Seeking Reconciliation*: Discovering the potential of reconciliation and the joy of restored relationship.

8. *Becoming the Beloved Community*: Embracing the power of forgiveness and reconciliation in our wider communities.

The Companions in Christ *Network*

An additional dimension of *Companions in Christ: The Way of Forgiveness* is the Network. While you and your group are experiencing *The Way of Forgiveness*, groups in other congregations will also be meeting. The Network provides opportunities for you to share your experiences with one another and to link in a variety of meaningful ways. In the Preparatory Meeting you will be invited to pray for another group, send greetings or encouragement, or receive their support for your group. Connecting in these ways will enrich your group's experience and the experience of those to whom you reach out.

The Network also provides a place for sharing conversation and information. The Companions Web site, www.companionsinchrist.org, includes a discussion room where you can offer insights, voice questions, and respond to others in an ongoing process of shared learning. The site provides a list of other groups using *The Way of Forgiveness* and their geographical locations so you can make connections as you feel led. Locations and dates for Leader Orientation training events (basic one-day trainings) and the Leader Training events (advanced three-day trainings) are posted here, and you will also find supplemental resource suggestions.

The *Companions* Network is a versatile and dynamic component of the *Companions in Christ* series. A Network toll free number (1-800-972-0433) is staffed during regular business hours.

The Role of the Small-Group Leader

Leading a group for spiritual formation differs in many ways from teaching a class. The most obvious difference comes in your basic goal as group leader. In a class you have particular information (facts, theories, ways of doing things) that you want to convey. You can gauge your success at the end of the class by participants' grasp of the information. In a group for spiritual formation, your goal is to enable spiritual growth in each group member. You work in partnership with the Holy Spirit, who alone can bring about transformation of the human heart. Here gaining wisdom is more important than gaining knowledge, and growing in holiness is more important than gaining either knowledge or wisdom. Success, if it has any meaning in this context, will be evident over months and even years in the changed lives of group members.

Classes tend to be task-oriented. Groups for spiritual formation tend to be more process-oriented. Even though group members will have done common preparation in reading and daily exercises, group discussions may move in directions you do not expect. You will need to be open to the movement of the Holy Spirit and vigilant in discerning the difference between following the Spirit's lead and going off on a tangent. Such discernment requires careful, prayerful listening. Listening will be much more important than talking in your role as group leader.

Finally, classes have as their primary focus some set of objective data. It could be a Bible passage, information from a book, or interpretations of current events. In a group for spiritual formation, however, the primary focus is on the personal faith experience of each group member. Each person seeks to understand and be open to the grace and revelation of God. Even when group members have read and reflected on a scripture passage, the basis for group discussion is not "What did the author intend to say to readers of that time?" but "How does this passage connect to my life or illumine my experience?" Discussion will be a sharing of experience, not a debate over ideas. You will model this type of personal sharing with the group because of your involvement in all parts of the learning process. The type of leadership needed differs from that of a traditional teacher of a church-school class or of a small-group facilitator. As the leader, you will read the material and complete the daily exercises along with other members and bring your responses to share with the group. You lead by offering your honest reflections and by trying to enable group members to listen carefully to one another and to the Spirit in your midst.

Leading a group for spiritual formation requires particular qualities. Foremost among these are patience and trust. You will need patience to allow the sessions to unfold as they will. Spiritual formation is a lifelong process. It may be difficult to identify any great leaps forward during the several weeks the group will spend on *The Way of Forgiveness*. It may even take a while for group members to adjust to the purpose and style of a formational group process. As a group leader, resolve that when you ask a question, you do not have a "right" answer in mind and that you really want participants to talk about their own experience. Setting an example of sharing your experience rather than proclaiming abstract truths or talking about the experiences of other well-known Christians will move along this shift from an informational approach to a formational process. Trust that the Holy Spirit will indeed help group members see or hear what they really need. You may offer what you consider a great insight to which no one responds. If it is what the group needs, the Spirit will bring it around again at a more opportune time. Susan Muto, a modern writer on spiritual formation, often says that we need to "make space for the pace of grace." There are no shortcuts to spiritual growth. Be patient and trust the Spirit.

Listening is another critical quality for a leader of a spiritual formation group. This does not mean simply listening for people to say what you hope they will say, so you can jump in and reinforce them. You need to listen for what is actually going on. What is actually happening in participants' minds and hearts may differ from what you expect after reading the material and doing the weekly exercises yourself. While you listen, you might want to jot down brief notes about themes that emerge in the discussion. Does a certain type of experience seem to be at the center of the sharing? Is a particular direction or common understanding emerging—a hint of God's will or a shared sense of what was especially helpful to several members of the group? Is there some action that group members need to take together or individually in order to move forward or to respond to an emerging sense of call? What do you hear again and again?

A group leader also needs to be accepting. Accept that group members may have had spiritual experiences quite unlike yours. Accept that people often see common experiences in dissimilar ways. Some may be struck by something that did not impress you at all, while others may be left cold by things that really excite or move you. As you model acceptance, you will help foster acceptance of one another's differences within the group. Beyond accepting differences, you will need to accept lack of closure. Group meetings will rarely tie up all the loose ends in a neat package. Burning questions will be left hanging. If important, they will surface again (which brings us back to patience and trust). Also be prepared to accept people's emotions along with their thoughts and experiences. Tears, fears, joy, and anger are to be received as legitimate responses along this journey. One important expression of acceptance is permission-giving. Permit people to grow and share at their own pace. Let group members know in your first meeting that while you want to encourage full participation in every part of the process, they are free to opt out of any experience or activity that makes them feel truly uncomfortable. No one will be forced to share or pray without consent. "Where the Spirit of the Lord is, there is freedom" (2 Cor. 3:17).

It is particularly important to avoid three common tendencies:

1. *Fixing.* When someone presents a specific problem, it will be tempting to want to find a solution and "fix" the problem. Problem solving generally makes us feel better. Perhaps it makes us feel wise or powerful or it helps to break the tension, but it will not help the other to grow. Moreover, you might prescribe the wrong fix! It is far better, if you have had a similar problem, to speak about your own experience and what worked for you. If you have not had direct experience, perhaps someone else in the group has.

2. *Proselytizing.* You know what has brought you closer to God. Naturally you would like everyone to try it. You can offer your own experience to the group, but it is dangerous spiritually to try to convince everyone to follow your path. Here is where your knowledge and wisdom come into play. Teresa of Avila wrote that if she had to choose between a director who was spiritual or one who was learned, she would pick the learned one.[1] The saint might be able to talk only about his or her own spiritual path. The learned one might at least recognize another person's experience from having read about such experiences. It is far more useful to be able to clarify and celebrate someone else's experience than to urge others to try to follow your way.

3. *Controlling.* Many of us are accustomed to filling in silence with some comment. It may be tempting to see ourselves as experts with an appropriate response to whatever anyone says; that is, we tend to dominate and control the conversation. Here again patience and listening are essential. Do not be afraid of silence. Your capacity to be comfortable with silence allows you to be a relaxed presence in the group. If you really cannot bear a long silence, it is better to break it with an invitation for someone (maybe someone who has been quiet so far) to share a thought, feeling, or question than with some comment of your own.

If this style of leadership seems challenging or unfamiliar to you, please seriously consider attending a leader training event for *Companions in Christ*. While leadership training is not required for this resource, it is highly recommended and strongly encouraged.

Expectations for the "Sharing Insights" Section of Each Meeting

This section offers a basic process for the first hour of your group session, the parts entitled "Opening" and "Sharing Insights" in the weekly format. The pattern that you follow during this time can be used for any small group for spiritual growth. In other groups you could substitute readings from a spiritual classic or meditations on selected passages of scripture for the readings and exercises in *Companions in Christ: The Way of Forgiveness*.

The first step in the group session is prayer and a time of quiet centering. Invoking the Holy Spirit's guiding presence is especially important in the "Opening," or gathering part of the weekly group meeting (see "A General Outline of Each Group Meeting," pages 21–23).

Most of the "Sharing Insights" part of the group session will focus on individual members talking about their experiences with the reading and daily exercises. Encourage members to bring their journals to refresh their memories of the week's exercises. As the leader, you will generally want to model by beginning with your own sharing. Your sharing sets the tone for the rest of the group. Make your sharing brief (two to three minutes) to allow ample time for others to share. Above all let it be specific, dealing with your response to one of the exercises. You need not announce a general topic. The rest of the group will have read the material and done the exercises. If your sharing is general or abstract, other participants will be less likely to share personal experiences. Your initial sharing in this part of the group meeting is one of your most important roles as the leader. Consider carefully each week what you would like to share, remaining mindful of how your sharing helps establish trust in the group as well as the serious intent of this part of the meeting.

During the "Sharing Insights" time, your main job is to listen. Listen primarily for themes—similar experiences that suggest a general truth about the spiritual life, common responses to the readings that might indicate a word God wants the group to hear, or recurring experiences that might offer practical help to other group members as they try to hear and respond to God's call. Take simple notes so you can lift up these themes as the "Sharing Insights" time comes to an end. You will also invite the other group members to share any themes or patterns they may have identified from the discussion. You can listen too for key differences in participants' experiences and affirm the variety of ways God speaks to and guides each one of us. You need to be alert to the temptation of participants to "fix" problems, proselytize, or control conversation. Gently remind them to share their own experiences or reactions. The same guidance applies if a participant mentions someone else as an example, whether in the group or outside it. Nothing can destroy group trust more quickly than exposing confidences.

By establishing up front some ground rules for group sharing, you may avoid problems. In the Preparatory Meeting, you will explain the various components of each week's meeting. It would be good to discuss the nature of this sharing time and establish some basic ground rules for the group. Here are some suggestions:

- Speak only for yourself about beliefs, feelings, and responses.

- Respect and receive what others offer, even if you disagree.

- Listening is more important than talking. Avoid cross talk, interrupting, speaking for others, or trying to "fix" another person's problems.

- Honor the different ways God works in individuals.

- Do not be afraid of silence. Use it to listen to the Spirit in your midst.

- Maintain confidentiality. What is shared in the group stays in the group (unless it has legal implications; this is not a "privileged" group legally).[2]

- Recognize that all group members have permission to share only what and when they are ready to share.

You may want to add to this list before you share it with the group.

A few minutes before the scheduled end of the group sharing session, state aloud any themes you have noted during the discussion: a summary report on what you have actually heard, not a chance to "get in the last word" on various topics of discussion. It can be fairly brief: "I noticed that several of us were especially drawn to a particular passage. I wonder if God is trying to call our attention to something here." Note: This is not a time for moving the discussion to a more abstract level but for summarizing and tying together some themes of the discussion that has already taken place.

Finally, you may want to close this part of the session with prayer. You may pray for the deepening of particular insights, for the ability to follow through on the themes or guidance you have heard, or for God's leading on questions that have been left open. You may feel a need to pray for particular situations that have been mentioned. And you may want to invite all group members who are willing to offer simple sentence prayers of their own.

A General Outline of Each Group Meeting

The weekly group meetings will typically follow the outline explained below. Within the outline are two overall movements: one primarily emphasizes sharing insight and learning from the week's reading and daily exercises; the other primarily develops a deeper understanding of spiritual disciplines or practices. The first movement, called "Sharing Insights," is a time of sharing and listening as described in the preceding section. The second part of the meeting, called "Deeper Explorations," may expand on ideas contained in the week's reading, offer practice in spiritual exercises being taught in the reading, or give group members a chance to reflect on the implications of what they are learning for their own journeys and for the church.

Both movements are intended as times of formation. In the first, the focus is on the group members' responses to the weekly reading and exercises. In the second, the focus is on expanding and deepening the content of the reading.

Consider carefully the setting for your group meetings. An adaptable space is important for group process. Most often the best arrangement is a circle of comfortable chairs or sofas. On occasion participants might want a surface for writing or drawing. Since the group will sometimes break into pairs or triads, space to separate is also important. The space for meeting will need to be relatively quiet and peaceful.

It is important to create a visual focus for the group, especially for opening and closing worship times. Some weeks you are free to create this in whatever way you may choose, perhaps using simply the Christ candle and a cloth on a small table in the center of the circle. However, several weekly sessions call for specific items. When this is the case, the items are listed for you under "Weekly Needs at a Glance" (pages 5–9) and the heading in the weekly outline "Prepare materials and meeting space." Some items are suggested to enrich the worship setting but are not specifically referred to during the meeting. For example, in Week 1, a robe (red if possible), ring, and sandals are placed on the worship table for the "Closing," but there is no discussion of them. Other items are woven into the content of the weekly session. In Week 4, for example, the Peace, Hope, and Justice prayer candle is introduced and explained; then it becomes part of the remaining weekly sessions without planned comment. It is strongly suggested that leaders review the "Prepare materials and meeting space" information for all eight weekly sessions prior to the Preparatory Meeting. Doing so will assure adequate time to gather, prepare, or purchase any items you may need.

OPENING (10 MINUTES)

This brief time of worship will give group members a chance to quiet down and prepare for the group session to follow. Each group will eventually discover what works best for its members. The Leader's Guide offers some specific suggestions, but you can develop your own pattern of prayer and centering, if you desire. Possibilities for this opening worship include (1) singing a hymn together, whether one that is sung at the beginning of every meeting or one that is specially selected each week; (2) silence; (3) lighting a candle; (4) scripture reading; (5) individual prayer, planned or extemporaneous; or (6) group prayer using a written or memorized prayer. Some hymns or songs that might be suitable for this beginning time are "Amazing Grace"; "Surely the Presence of the Lord"; "Sweet, Sweet Spirit"; "Spirit Song"; "Sanctuary"; "Lord, Be Glorified"; "Into My Heart"; and "Ubi Caritas."

SHARING INSIGHTS (45 MINUTES)

The content for this part of the meeting comes from the weekly reading and from participants' responses to the five daily exercises that they have completed since the last meeting. If members fail to read the material or skip the daily exercises, they will be left out. If too many come unprepared, the group process simply will not work. Group interaction generally will follow the model given above under "Expectations for the 'Sharing Insights' Section of Each Meeting." Since the "Opening" has provided prayer and centering time, this section would begin with your own sharing as the group leader, continue with group interaction, and end with whatever summary you feel is helpful, followed by a brief prayer. You will need to keep an eye on the time in order to bring the sharing to a close and have time for summary and prayer.

BREAK (10 MINUTES)

Group break time serves several important purposes physically, mentally, and relationally. It also gives some time for snacking if you arrange for someone to provide food. Do not neglect or squeeze out adequate break time, and be sure to take a break yourself as leader.

DEEPER EXPLORATIONS (45 MINUTES)

This part of the group meeting builds on material in the weekly reading and daily exercises. The content for this time takes three primary forms. It may expand on the reading through discussion of related materials. It may apply the reading through exercises, relating its content to the lives of individual members, to the life of the group as a whole, or to the church. Finally, it may offer further practice in the disciplines explored in the reading or exercises, either by going through a similar exercise in the group or by presenting alternative ways of practicing these disciplines. This segment of the meeting is very important. It is like the experiential part of a spiritual retreat in miniature and requires your thoughtful preparation as the leader if you are to guide the process comfortably. Please review the leader material early in the week prior to the meeting so that you have time to think through the process and complete any preparation.

CLOSING (10 MINUTES)

As it began, the group meeting ends with a time of simple worship. First you may need to attend to practical matters of meeting place or provision of refreshments if these vary from week to week. You may also draw names for prayer partners for the coming week and ask for prayer requests.

The Leader's Guide includes suggestions for the "Closing." Several of these are specifically designed to bring closure to the particular content of a given week's "Deeper Explorations." However, if you choose to develop your own plans, consider the following ideas: the time of closing worship may include intercessions for special requests, prayers that flow from the content of the group's meeting, and any other prayers group members feel led to offer. You may want to finish with the Lord's Prayer to place these specific prayers in the content of the universal prayer of Christ's church. You may want to conclude the entire meeting with a hymn or song. Here are some appropriate ones: "Blest Be the Tie That Binds"; "Sent Forth by God's Blessing"; "Shalom to You"; "Lord, Dismiss Us with Thy Blessing"; "God Be with You till We Meet Again"; or the "Companion Song."

Concluding Matters

With larger groups (10–12) or groups that appreciate a more contemplative pace, you may need more than one week to work through the materials and experiences under a given topic. In this case feel free to negotiate with your members for an extended meeting time or to take two weeks for one topic.

Issues of forgiveness and reconciliation can lead people into deep waters, both spiritually and emotionally. As a group leader, you may discover on occasion that a participant needs support beyond the scope of the group. Remember that the purpose of this group is not therapy but Christian formation. Some unhealed wounds may require the help of a trained counselor or spiritual director. It is important for you to know when to refer a group member to a church staff person or lay member with counseling expertise. Think in advance about a few persons you could recommend to a group member if necessary, and ask if they would be willing to be contacted.

Here are a few signs that can help you identify when to refer:

- You feel "out of your depth" responding to a deeply personal issue that is divulged.
- One individual is beginning to dominate sharing time around a personal problem.
- A participant shares a profoundly disturbing spiritual or psychic experience that leaves the group uneasy.
- A participant becomes unusually emotional or withdrawn for several weeks.

Some persons feel more anxious than others about sharing personal stories, and are more sensitive to issues of confidentiality. If, after working through your small-group ground rules, you find that someone is still uncertain about entrusting the group with personal sharing, you might consider using the following prayers for "Opening" and "Closing" times in the first week.

> These two prayers were composed by a woman who was terrified by the thought that someone in the group with which she would share her story would desecrate it by violating confidentiality. By praying these prayers in unison, she and others were enabled to trust and share honestly their fragile autobiographies.

Prayer for Openness

Author of all our stories, who imagined us into being,
    be with us as we share the plots of our lives.
Create a sacred space where the words we speak
    will be heard with compassion, not judgment.
Remind us to reveal only as much of the mystery of who we are
    as we feel comfortable disclosing.
Help us to read between the lines of each other's lives
    and see the themes that connect each scene together.
Keep us from the temptation to tell each other's stories,
    or to use anything that is said today against one another.
Thank you for the opportunity to know who you are
    as we discover your incarnation in each other.
Amen.

Prayer for Closure

Creator of us all, we see you in each other's eyes,
    hear you in each other's words,
    learn who you are as we learn to understand ourselves.
Help us to leave this space feeling whole, not broken;
    healed, not wounded;
    loved, not despised.
We have experienced the sacrament of sharing our stories,
    and promise to keep them sacred.
Amen.[3]

The Leader's Guide on occasion suggests songs for certain meetings, but they are only suggestions. Each group will have access to different hymnals and songbooks and will have its own preference in musical style. The Participant's Book (pages 114–115) includes a song written specifically for *Companions in Christ*, called "Companion Song." It includes annotations both for piano and guitar accompaniment. The music is simple to learn, and the song could serve as a theme song for your group. We encourage you to try it in your Preparatory Meeting and to use it a few times during your early meetings. If the group members like it, they will naturally ask to sing it as you move through these weeks together.

The purpose of the *Companions in Christ* series is to equip persons of faith with both personal and corporate spiritual life practices that will continue long beyond the time frame of this particular resource. Participants may continue certain disciplines on their own or carry some practices into congregational life. Others may desire the continuation of a small group. You will likely discover, as you guide your group through this eight-week journey, that certain topics generate interest and energy for further exploration. Some group members may wish that certain readings or weekly meetings could go into more depth. When the group expresses strong desire to continue with a particular topic or practice, take special note of it. A number of possibilities exist for small-group study and practice beyond this resource. Some suggested resources are listed on pages 103–108 of the Participant's Book.

Our prayer for you as a leader is that the weeks ahead will lead you and your group deeper into the heart and mind, the work and spirit, the very life of Jesus Christ. May your companionship with Christ and with one another be richly blessed.

Preparatory Meeting

The Leader's Guide to *Companions in Christ: The Way of Forgiveness* addresses you directly as the leader concerning most of the material in each group meeting. In places the Leader's Guide also offers suggested words for you to speak to the group as a way of introducing various sections. Where this occurs, the words are printed in a light bold typeface (such as the first item under "Introduce the Study"). Be assured that these words are only suggestions. Always feel free to express the same idea in your own words or adapt it as you deem necessary.

PREPARATION

Prepare yourself spiritually. Review the material in the Introduction to the Participant's Book, as well as the information in the Leader's Guide Introduction. Look over the Contents page in the Participant's Book so you can answer questions that may arise. Pray for each group member and for the beginning of this journey together as companions in Christ. Also pray that God will guide you in your role as leader so that the small group might begin this time together with openness and genuine expectation.

Prepare materials and meeting space. You will need a "talking piece" (information on pages 30–31); marker and flip chart or other large piece of paper with group ground rules written out in advance; a printout from the "Way of Forgiveness Groups" area of the Web site www.companionsinchrist.org, which lists groups with whom you may wish to partner; and the card "Prayer for Our *Companions in Christ* Group"(in the back of this leader's guide). Arrange for hymnals or songbooks. Select the hymns or songs that you want to use for the "Opening" and "Closing." Review the scripture text for the opening worship.

Set up chairs in a circle with a center table and Christ candle. Make sure you have a copy of the Participant's Book for each person.

Review the intent of this meeting: that participants will have a clear understanding of the purpose and process of *Companions in Christ: The Way of Forgiveness.* Be sure participants have an opportunity to express their questions as well as their hopes for the eight-week journey. Participants should also see and have a chance to agree to the guidelines the group will observe.

OPENING (10 MINUTES)

Welcome all participants by name as they enter.

Introduce the study.

- **This meeting is preparation for your participation in a new venture called *Companions in Christ: The Way of Forgiveness.***

- **It is a small-group resource in spiritual formation that will lead us through an eight-week pilgrimage with Christ into the fullness of God's blessing.**

- **As companions in Christ, we will venture into the wildernesses of shame, guilt, and anger; face the challenges of receiving forgiveness, forgiving others, and seeking reconciliation; and emerge, by grace, a step closer to becoming participants in God's beloved community.**

Introduce the people.

- Ask group members to introduce themselves by saying their name, the church they belong to, and one other thing about themselves that is important to them.

- As leader, begin by introducing yourself in this way. Then invite others to follow your lead and introduce themselves.

Join together in worship.

- **Before we talk through a number of items, let's take a brief time to worship together, bringing ourselves and this venture before God in prayer.**

- Light a candle as a symbol of the presence of Christ's light in our midst and say, **Whenever we gather, we are together in the living presence of the Risen Lord, Jesus Christ.**

- Read Psalm 51:10-12.

- Take a moment of silence, and encourage participants to pray for the gifts named in this psalm.

- Offer prayer for openness of mind and heart to the guiding grace of the Holy Spirit for the journey ahead, and for God's blessing on each person and on the whole group.

- Introduce the "Companion Song" or sing a song or hymn such as "Give Me a Clean Heart."

PRESENT THE RESOURCES AND GROUP PROCESS (10 MINUTES)

Introduce the group process.

If you have not yet done so, hand out the Participant's Books. Be familiar with the material in the introduction to the Participant's Book and the Leader's Guide. Go over the content with group members so that each person understands the process of reading, daily exercises and journaling, as well as the outline for each group meeting. Here are some items you will want to mention:

Basic flow of the week. Each participant reads the article for the week on Day 1 (the day after the group meeting) and works through the five daily exercises over Days 2–6. The group meets on Day 7. Encourage participants to be faithful to the process and suggest that in preparation for the group meeting they read over their notebooks/journals for the week after doing the fifth daily exercise.

Basic flow of a group meeting. Explain the various components: "Opening" (akin to our opening worship time), "Sharing Insights," "Deeper Explorations," and "Closing." Summarize for the group the explanatory material found in "A General Outline of Each Group Meeting" on pages 21–23 of the Introduction to the Leader's Guide.

Materials for each meeting. Ask the members to bring Bibles, their Participant's Books, and their journals to each meeting. Because they will be using the Bible as part of the daily exercises, you may want to encourage persons to use a modern translation with study aids, or the Spiritual Formation Bible.

EXPLAIN PARTICIPANT RESPONSIBILITIES (15 MINUTES)

Emphasize the importance of each member's commitment to daily exercises for the group process to work. Because some members will not have experienced this type of group interaction, you may need to help them feel comfortable with it by explaining the basic simplicity of this model of sharing with one another. Remind them that one of the ways we listen to God is to put our experience into words. The process of articulation often brings clarity and new perspective. Therefore the group becomes a space for deep listening and trusting in God's guiding presence.

Introduce the "talking piece."

The "talking piece" illustrates the kind of respectful sharing and prayerful listening that characterizes our time together as companions in Christ.

The "talking piece" as a way of sharing and listening

The "talking piece" is a Native American way of helping us honor each speaker with a listening ear. It also ensures that everyone has a chance to speak without interruption. The "talking piece" is placed on the floor or table in the center of the group, where we might imagine Christ stands in our midst. When anyone wants to speak, he or she takes up the "talking piece," returning it to the center when finished. No one speaks unless holding the "talking piece." The group listens for the wisdom of God in and through each speaker. Many different items can serve as the "talking piece": a stick, a cross, a Bible, or another meaningful object. As leader, select an item that you think will have significance to the group.

Lead the group in a round of sharing using the "talking piece" method.

- Invite people to reflect on and be prepared to say a word about why they have come to be part of this eight-week journey. What are their hopes and expectations?

- Give the members a few minutes to reflect in silence. Ask them to jot down responses in their notebooks or journals.

- As leader, initiate the sharing. Place the "talking piece" in the middle of the group, pick it up to initiate the sharing, then ask others to follow.

- When all have shared in this way, ask group members to reflect for a moment on what the experience was like.

- Make it clear that while the "talking piece" will not necessarily be used in the sessions that follow (unless the group chooses to do so), it illustrates the intended quality of sharing and listening.

DISCUSS COMMON GROUND RULES (15 MINUTES)

Present some common ground rules such as the ones you have listed on newsprint from page 20 in the Introduction to the Leader's Guide.

- Ask participants to reflect in silence on the ground rules that are more and less important for them, and to consider other ground rules or agreements they would cherish. Direct them to jot down their thoughts in their notebooks or journals.

- Invite group members to share their thoughts.

- List on newsprint any new ideas suggested and embraced by the group. The goal is not a formal agreement or covenant but an appreciation for the kinds of ground rules that are essential and that group members are prepared to respect.

- Direct people's attention to the paragraph in the Participant's Book Introduction indicating the limits and responsibilities of a *Companions in Christ: The Way of Forgiveness* group (page 16).

JOURNALING (5 MINUTES)

Note that participants may have already been exercising an important practice for the course: journaling. Call their attention to pertinent points from the material on pages 12–14 of the Participant's Book about the value of recording reflections in a journal or personal notebook. Assure them that the writing can be as informal and unstructured as they want. Each person will keep whatever notes are most helpful for him or her, and the journal becomes the personal record of the spiritual growth that this resource is designed to encourage.

INTRODUCE THE *COMPANIONS IN CHRIST* NETWORK AND PRAYER CONNECTIONS (5 MINUTES)

Although we are focused on what is happening in our group, it is important for us to remember that many other groups across the country are participating in *Companions in Christ* also. We can communicate and be connected with those groups who are on the same spiritual journey in ways that strengthen our bonds in the body of Christ. We have two opportunities to link with others:

- *Correspondence with other groups.* Look for the link to *The Way of Forgiveness Groups* on the *Companions in Christ* Web site (www.companionsinchrist.org). Print out a list of *Way of Forgiveness* groups with whom you might partner. You can search by city, state, denomination, and other key words. Encourage your members to select and partner with a group, perhaps communicating through letters of greeting, encouragement or by sending a small love-gift. While at this site, you may wish to add your group to the list.

- Also the Upper Room Living Prayer Center and its network of prayer volunteers will begin to hold your group in prayer. Simply fill in and mail the card entitled "Prayer for Our *Companions in Christ* Group" that is bound into the Leader's Guide. Complete the leader's portion of the card by providing your name and your church's mailing address. Please do not use a post office box number. Ask each member of the group to sign his or her first name as evidence of the group's desire to be connected to the larger network of persons involved in *Companions in Christ*.

CLOSING (10 MINUTES)

Remind the members of their weekly assignment. The first day they will read the article "Living in God's Blessing." Each of the next five days they will work through one exercise and record their thoughts in their journal. Also be sure all participants know the location and time of the next meeting and any special responsibilities (such as providing snacks or helping to arrange the worship table).

Invite a time of quiet reflection. **What are your hopes for the time ahead of us as companions in Christ?…What are your anxieties about this time?…Commit both your hopes and your fears to God in silent prayer now.…**

Offer a brief word of prayer, asking that you all might be able to release your hopes and concerns into God's good and gracious hands. End with thanksgiving for each person and for God's good purposes in bringing this group together.

Say or sing a benediction such as "Go Now in Peace" or "Shalom to You."

Week 1
Living in God's Blessing

PREPARATION

Prepare yourself spiritually. Review the material in the Introduction of this Leader's Guide to remind yourself of key principles in small-group spiritual formation and your role in guiding it. Read the article for Week 1, do all the exercises, and keep your journal. Pray for each participant and for your ability to be present to the Spirit in this meeting time.

Prepare materials and the meeting space. Set chairs in a circle around a center worship table on which you place a candle. Have enough hymnals or songbooks to share; select songs for the "Opening" and "Closing." Bring a few extra Bibles. Obtain a robe (red if possible), ring, and sandals and place them on the worship table. Cut the reproduction of Rembrandt's painting *Return of the Prodigal Son* from the back of your Participant's Book and prop it up on the table as well. Write out the group litany response on a sheet of newsprint reserved for the "Closing."

Review the intent of this meeting: that participants come to a fuller appreciation of God's blessing in their lives and of the journey before them so that they might live into the fullness of God's blessing.

OPENING (10 MINUTES)

Welcome all participants by name as they enter.

Set a context.

- This meeting is the first session of eight designed to help us learn the way of forgiveness in the Christian life. In this first meeting, we will explore God's blessing in our lives and the call to live into the fullness of that blessing.

- Take a few minutes to renew bonds or get better acquainted with one another. Invite group members to say their names and one thing they remember as a child about church or an impression of the church they carry from childhood.

Join together in worship.

- **We light a candle to symbolize the presence of the light of Christ in our midst each time we gather. May the wisdom and enlightenment of the Holy Spirit be our guide throughout this exploration of the way of forgiveness.**

- Read 1 John 3:1-3. Reread verse 2, emphasizing what we already are "now" and what we "will be" that is not yet revealed.

- Offer a brief prayer of thanks for the privilege of being together and for the gifts we trust God desires to give to each person here during these next eight weeks. Pray for open minds and hearts to receive these gifts so we can in turn share them.

- Sing a song of praise, thanks, or blessing. Suggestions: "Give Thanks," "Count Your Blessings."

SHARING INSIGHTS (45 MINUTES)

In this part of the meeting, group members will identify and share where they have experienced God's presence in their lives this past week. Begin by reminding group members of the theme for this week—that we are blessed as we live by the patterns of Christ's life.

1. Give participants a few minutes to review the article for this week and their journal entries that accompany the daily exercises. (*5 minutes*)

2. Ask participants to share insights from the weekly reading and their journal entries. As leader, model the sharing by offering your own brief reflections first. Encourage deep and active listening, reminding the group of last week's "talking piece" exercise. If the group numbers more than eight, you may want to break into two groups to ensure that everyone can participate in the sharing. (*35 minutes*)

3. With the whole group, draw out the main points or common themes that emerged from their discussion. What refrains or echoes were evident in these shared reflections? (*5 minutes*)

BREAK (10 MINUTES)

DEEPER EXPLORATIONS (45 MINUTES)

Note: As the leader, you may wish to review the process of biblical meditation or lectio divina *for yourself (see the Leader's Notes). You will be guiding group* lectio *in this part of the meeting. There is no need to introduce participants to the process at this point. Simply let them experience it. You might note before the "Closing" that this approach to scripture will be used with variations throughout these eight weeks.*

Introduce the theme. (3 minutes)

You may use words like these: **We will be contemplating the blessed life that God gives us through Jesus Christ and what it tells us about our journey along the way of forgiveness. The image we will use to help us contemplate the blessed life in relation to forgiveness is a famous Rembrandt painting,** *Return of the Prodigal Son* **(reproductions found in the back of the Participant's Book and on the worship table).**

Prepare to meditate on Luke 15:11-32 and Return of the Prodigal Son *painting. (5 minutes)*

- Both the painting and the story illustrate broadly the way of forgiveness.

- Indicate that we have here a threefold picture: our great need to receive God's blessing and all-forgiving love (the prodigal son), the call to embody the compassion of God in our relations with others (the father), and the great difficulty we experience in doing any of this (the elder son, standing to the right with illumined face in Rembrandt's painting).

- Invite group members to contemplate the painting as they listen to the story.

- If you have a group of 10–12 members, you may wish to form two or three clusters for the shared responses that follow each reading.

Read Luke 15:11-32, first reading. (5 minutes)

Prior to the first reading, ask the group simply to pay attention to and write down the word, phrase, or image that captures their attention in a special way.

- Read the text without rushing.

- Allow a minute of silence for pondering.

- Invite each person who so desires to share the word, phrase, or image heard (no expanded discussion at this time).

Read Luke 15:11-32, second reading. (12 minutes)

Before reading, provide a transition using the following quote by Henri Nouwen:

> It was so easy to identify with the two sons. Their outer and inner waywardness is so understandable and so profoundly human that identification happens almost spontaneously.[1]

Invite participants to focus on the two sons (in the story and in the painting) and to notice, as they listen and ponder, the one with whom they most identify and why.

- Read the text.

- Allow a few minutes of silent reflection.

- Invite brief sharing of how each person senses identification (no discussion).

Read Luke 15:11-32, third reading. (20 minutes)

Prior to reading, continue with Nouwen's quote:

> But…why talk so much about being like the sons when the real question is: Are you interested in being like the father?…Do I want to be not just the one who is being forgiven, but also the one who forgives; not just the one who is being welcomed home, but also the one who welcomes home; not just the one who receives compassion, but the one who offers it as well?[2]

Ask the group to focus on the father (in the story and the painting) and to pay attention to what they see, hear, and feel.

- Read the text once more.

- Invite participants to ponder quietly where they have seen or experienced what they see in the father and to jot down thoughts in their journals. Allow a few minutes of silence.

- Invite group members to dialogue on the whole story and to share their learnings.

CLOSING (10 MINUTES)

Prepare for worship. Be sure the Rembrandt reproduction is visible on the center worship table alongside symbols of the story: sandals, ring, and robe. Place the group litany response on newsprint where all can see it. Light the Christ candle (if it has been extinguished) and allow a few moments of quiet for people to absorb what they have received and will carry with them from the meeting time.

Invite reflection and response:

- Ask participants to reflect on the symbolic significance of the robe, ring, and sandals. They are signs of dignity, authority, and freedom that the father bestows on *both* sons.

- Ask, **What was the gift and the challenge of this time for you?** After a minute of silence, invite brief responses.

Offer a closing litany of prayer. Indicate the group response to each prayer phrase (written on newsprint).

Prayer Litany

Leader: O God, while we were still far off, you saw us and ran to embrace us!
Group: May we grow into your loving likeness.

Leader: O Christ, we have been lost, but now by your love we are found!
Group: May we grow into your loving likeness.

Leader: O Holy Spirit, we were dead, but now by your grace are alive!
Group: May we grow into your loving likeness.

Leader: May we enter humbly into your joy, Great God.
Group: May we grow into your loving likeness.

Leader: Hear this gracious assurance from our Lord:
"You are always with me; all that I have is yours."
Such is the generous blessing of our God
and we are deeply grateful. Amen.

Say or sing a benediction.

Leader's Notes

MEDITATION ON SCRIPTURE (*LECTIO DIVINA*)

What is the process? We start by *reading* a Bible passage to take in its content and contours, to hear the words clearly and to observe the characters in action. We go on to *reflect* on possible meanings and to ponder connections with our lived experience in the world. Then we *respond* in prayer, sharing our thoughts with God and listening for God to speak to us. Finally, we *rest* in the word or grace that God gives us, acknowledging what we have received with thanksgiving. (This acknowledgment will normally lead to a step beyond the time of meditation in which we offer our active response.)

The process can and should take many creative forms, depending on the passage and who is listening. Yet the basic elements of the process remain fairly constant as trustworthy means of searching beyond the surface of scripture and opening our lives to the searchlight of God's love. The daily exercises call us to meditate on scripture in relation to daily life and the themes of this course. The weekly meetings continue this dynamic as we share together the "daily bread" God gives us and as we practice scriptural meditation and listening prayer in company with one another.

THE RETURN OF THE PRODIGAL SON

The painting *Return of the Prodigal Son* is the product of Rembrandt's meditation on the biblical story in relation to his own tumultuous life. It is more than a depiction of a Bible story. On this canvas he portrays his interior vision of the story's meaning—the all-forgiving compassion of God and the struggles of people to accept and share such love. The artist painted this masterpiece near the end of his life. Some interpreters believe it represents a spiritual self-portrait. Aspects of Rembrandt's life pilgrimage are visible in each of the three central characters in the painting.

The painting embodies meditation on scripture. The aim of pondering and praying God's word over the course of a lifetime is that we gain a deepening interior vision of God and how we live our lives daily in and through Jesus Christ, the Word made flesh.

Week 2

Releasing Shame and Guilt

PREPARATION

Prepare yourself spiritually. Review once more the portions of the Leader's Guide relevant to your role as small-group leader. Pray for grace to be open to the Holy Spirit's guidance in your preparation and meeting time. Read the weekly article, do all the daily exercises, and keep your journal. Review this week's meeting process carefully.

Prepare materials and the meeting space. Arrange chairs in a circle with a center table and candle. Gather your hymnals or songbooks. Select songs for the "Opening" and "Closing." Make copies for each group member of the "Meditation with John 11" (pages 46–47 of the Leader's Guide). Obtain a stone and a long strip of cloth for each person in the group, including you. The strips should be about 2–3 feet long by 1 inch wide and could be torn from an old sheet or flour sack dish towel. You will need a container for the stones, such as a bucket, sturdy basket, or bowl.

Review the intent of this meeting: that participants come to a deeper experience of freedom from the bondage of shame and guilt, the freedom made available to them by faith in Christ.

OPENING (10 MINUTES)

Welcome all participants personally as they enter.

Set a context.

This meeting is the second of eight in our exploration of the way of forgiveness. We are looking this week at what prevents us from experiencing fully our God-blessed identity. Shame and guilt are the chief blocks, along with all the patterns of life that lead to them and hold them in place. Our meeting will give us time to look at these blocks and hopefully to discover a new sense of freedom in relation to them.

Join together in worship.

- **Listen to the following verses of Psalm 25. As you listen, notice which of the psalmist's experiences of shame or guilt you can personally identify with as a result of doing the daily exercises this week.** (Read slowly.)

  To you, O LORD, I lift up my soul.
  O my God, in you I trust;
      do not let me be put to shame;…
  Be mindful of your mercy, O LORD,
      and of your steadfast love,
    for they have been from of old.
  Do not remember the sins of my youth
      or my transgressions;
    according to your steadfast love remember me,
    for your goodness' sake, O LORD!…
  Turn to me and be gracious to me,
    for I am lonely and afflicted.
  Relieve the troubles of my heart,
    and bring me out of my distress.…
  May integrity and uprightness preserve me,
    for I wait for you.

- Invite silent reflection for a few minutes. Then encourage participants to turn to one other person and share the words or phrases from the psalm they could identify with and (if they wish) why.

- Sing a song or hymn celebrating God's goodness and kindness toward us. Suggestions: "Amazing Grace"; "O How I Love Jesus"; "Savior, Like a Shepherd Lead Us."

- Close with a simple prayer of thanksgiving and praise.

SHARING INSIGHTS (45 MINUTES)

In this portion of the meeting group members identify and share where they have experienced God's presence in their lives this past week. Begin by reminding group members of this week's theme: releasing shame and guilt. The daily exercises for this week are aimed at helping participants get in touch both with the reality of shame and guilt that become obstacles to the blessed life and with the reality of God's acceptance and grace in their lives, gifts that restore the blessing.

1. Allow a brief time for participants to review this week's article and the journal entries that accompany the daily exercises. (*5 minutes*)

2. Ask participants to share with one another insights from the reading and from their journal entries. As leader, model the quality of sharing by offering your own brief reflections first. Encourage active and deep listening during this time. (*35 minutes*)

3. Leave some time to help the group recover main points or common themes that have emerged in the sharing of insights. What patterns, if any, may be discerned? (*5 minutes*)

BREAK (10 MINUTES)

DEEPER EXPLORATIONS (40 MINUTES)

Introduce the theme—exploring how Christ raises us from our "living deaths" and calls us to participate in the raising of one another. (*5 minutes*)

- We know that we are blessed and called, as God's beloved and forgiven children, to walk in the way that leads to life. Yet the shame and guilt we carry with us from the past can entomb us in a living death.

- In the prodigal son story, the father exclaimed, "This my son was lost and now is found, was dead and now is alive!" Once the son decided to return, the father's love overcame the young man's shame and guilt and raised him from what could have been a living death—a life completely defined, entombed by past mistakes.

- Christ is in the business of overcoming deaths of every kind in our lives.

- The story of the raising of Lazarus invites us to consider, while our bodies still have breath, where we are already dead and need to be raised to new life.

- When we read the story, we can see that Jesus did not accomplish the raising of Lazarus in isolation but with the cooperation of the faith community.

Involve the group in a participatory reading of John 11:1-44. (*10 minutes*)

- Assign members of the group a role in the story to read. Make sure all are reading from the same translation of the Bible. The potential parts include Jesus, his disciples, Thomas,

Martha, Mary, the Jews, Lazarus, and the narrator. Combine parts as needed. As group leader, take the role of narrator, reading all parts of the story other than those you assign to others.

- Read the passage as a group.

- After the reading ask participants to name a word or phrase that stayed with them.

Solitary reflection on the story of Lazarus. (*15 minutes*)

- Encourage each participant to find some personal space.

- Instruct participants to take their Bibles and to follow the guidelines for reflection on the sheet called "Meditation with John 11" (hand out the sheets).

- Indicate that you will ring a bell or call out at the end of 15 minutes, a signal for them to return to the group.

Sharing in clusters (10 minutes)

- Form clusters of 3–4 people.

- Ask participants to listen to one another as they share insights into the passage in relation to their own lives.

CLOSING (15 MINUTES)

On the worship table place the container of stones and a wad of old binding (the strips of cloth bundled together).

Pass the container around and let participants take from it what they choose to represent their sense of being blocked or bound.

Read this quote from Charles Williams:

> If you want to disobey and refuse the laws that are common to us all, if you want to live in pride and division and anger, you can. But if you will be part of the best of us, and live and laugh and be ashamed with us, then you must be content to be helped. You must give your burden up to someone else, and you must carry someone else's burden. I haven't made the universe and it isn't my fault. But I'm sure that this is a law of the universe, and not to give up your parcel is as much to rebel as not to carry another's. You'll find it quite easy if you let yourself do it.[1]

Invite group members to a time of silent prayer.

- **As we have seen in the story of Lazarus, the fullness of our liberation from bondage occurs within community, not just "between me and God."**

- Guide the prayer time by asking participants to consider what obstacle in their lives (stone or binding) they need God's help or the help of loving friends to get past.

- After a minute or so of silent meditation, invite them to go forward quietly to place their stone or binding on the worship table. They may place it on the table in silence, or they may say a word or phrase to indicate the nature of their need. Go first to model the action.

- After everyone who chooses to has gone forward, invite the group to a time of intercessory prayer for those places or people where Christ calls for our assistance to roll away a stone or remove whatever binds.

Sing "Precious Lord, Take My Hand."

Offer a closing benediction.

Meditation with John 11

THE RAISING OF LAZARUS

Read chapter 11:1-44 to review the story.

So the sisters sent a message to Jesus, "Lord, he whom you love is ill."…Accordingly, though Jesus loved Martha and her sister and Lazarus, after having heard that Lazarus was ill, he stayed two days longer in the place where he was.

The story tells us several times of Jesus' love for his friends. Pause for a few prayerful moments to abide in Jesus' love, alongside Martha and Mary and Lazarus.

What do you need to do to be steeped more deeply in Jesus' love?

Jesus said, "Take away the stone."

What is the most urgent place where you are bound or live in deadness from which Christ calls you out?

Martha, the sister of the dead man, said to him, "Lord, already there is a stench...."

The shame or guilt we carry rarely affects only us. What is the "stench" of your situation that affects others as well as yourself?

He cried with a loud voice, "Lazarus, come out!"
What would it mean for you to "come out" and be alive in Jesus' love?

Jesus said to them, "Unbind him, and let him go."
What is the most urgent place where Christ wants your assistance in calling forth a person or group from being bound, from deadness?

Facing Our Anger

PREPARATION

Prepare yourself spiritually. Review the introductory material in the Leader's Guide again if you would find this helpful. Read the article for Week 3, do all the exercises, and keep your journal notes. Pray for each participant and for your own openness to God as you lead the group.

Prepare materials and the meeting space. Review the process for this week's meeting. Select any hymns or songs you wish to use, and have sufficient songbooks or hymnals at hand. Set chairs in a circle with a center table, candle, and any other appropriate symbols you may wish to add. Bring colored markers or crayons for use in the "Deeper Explorations."

Review the intent of this meeting: that participants gain clarity about various faces of anger, the sources of anger, and anger's impact for good or ill in our lives.

OPENING (10 MINUTES)

Welcome all participants personally as they enter.

Set a context.

We are beginning to explore the nature of anger in our lives, how we experience it, where we see it, and how as people of faith we might best deal with its reality. Our anger can be scary and disturbing. It can also be empowering. We do well to begin our consideration of this subject by coming before God in worship.

Join together in worship.

- Light a candle as a sign of seeking the light of God's wisdom and affirming the truth of Christ's presence with the group.

- Sing a meditative song or chant that invites people to open their spirits to the gracious Spirit of God. Suggestions: "Holy, Holy, Holy" (Argentine folk version), "Take, O Take" (Iona), a Taizé chant, or a meditative Alleluia.

- Slowly read the following passage: "Be angry but do not sin; do not let the sun go down on your anger, and do not make room for the devil" (Eph. 4:26-27). After a pause, read it again without rushing. Invite a few minutes of quiet reflection to listen to what the Spirit is saying to each person and to the group in these words.

- Invite participants to offer one-sentence prayers based on what they are hearing. Close by offering a brief prayer asking for God's wisdom and truth to speak to the hearts of all present, and for the willingness to continue listening deeply to the Spirit and to one another.

SHARING INSIGHTS (45 MINUTES)

For the next 45 minutes, group members will have an opportunity to identify and share where they have experienced God's presence in their lives this past week. Begin by reminding group members of the theme for this week: facing our anger. The article for this week introduces the idea of anger and discusses various kinds of anger we typically experience. The daily exercises for this week help group members examine some of their own experiences of anger through the guidance of key biblical passages.

1. Ask participants to take a few minutes to look over the article for the week as well as their journal entries based on the daily exercises. (*5 minutes*)

2. Ask participants to share their insights from the weekly reading and/or from their journal entries for the week. As the leader, model the sharing by offering your brief reflections first. Encourage active and deep listening during this sharing time. (*35 minutes*)

3. Conclude this time by bringing out the main points or common themes from the previous discussion. What patterns emerged in the sharing time? (*5 minutes*)

BREAK (10 MINUTES)

DEEPER EXPLORATIONS (45 MINUTES)

Set a context. (*2 minutes*) As we work on *facing* our anger, it may help to consider the *faces* of anger we see in ourselves and in the world. The story in Mark's Gospel of Jesus healing the man with the withered hand presents us with three distinct "faces of anger." By entering into this story, we may gain greater clarity about the nature and character of anger in our lives and deeper perspective on destructive and constructive anger.

Prepare to lead a guided meditation with scripture. (3 minutes)

Invite group members to find a position that helps them to be both alert and relaxed. Ask them to invite the Holy Spirit to guide their minds and hearts in this reflective process. Assure them that they have freedom to participate fully or to opt out of any part they are uncomfortable with, but encourage them to give it a try. Indicate that if any have difficulty with visualizing, they may simply use thought, intuition, or sensing to help them enter the story. They might also wish to write words or phrases that come to mind or use colors to express what they perceive and feel (be sure colored markers or crayons are within easy reach of participants).

Read Mark 3:1-6, first reading, followed by sharing. (10 minutes)

Before reading, invite the group members as they listen to reflect on where they see anger in this story: in whom and toward what?

• *Read the story at a pace that allows for reflective listening.*

• *Allow a minute of silence for group members to contemplate what they see.*

• *Ask,* **Where do you see the face of anger in this story (for example, in the Pharisee, in Jesus, or even in the man with the withered hand)?** *Invite brief sharing.*

Read Mark 3:1-6, second reading, followed by quiet reflection. (15 minutes)

• Tell the group you will be reading the story again, then guiding a brief meditation that focuses first on the Pharisees and then on Jesus.

• Read the story again.

• Guide the meditation:

  Close your eyes and visualize or sense the presence of the Pharisees in the story....What do you see and feel?...

  Take a few minutes to draw a sketch, symbol, or color in your journal expressing what you see and feel.... *(Allow a few minutes.)* Indicate that the participants may also want to jot down words or phrases that describe what they perceive, and remind them that they need not share these unless they choose to.

Now reflect on where you see the same kind of anger in yourself. Do you see your face in any of their faces, and if so, how?…If you have difficulty finding a connection, reflect on where you see this kind of anger in your church, community, or world.…Note any insights in your journal. (*Allow a few minutes.*)

Close your eyes again and visualize or sense the presence of Jesus in the story.…What do you see and feel?…

Take a few minutes to draw a mark, color, or symbol of what you see and feel.… (*Allow a few minutes.*)

Where do you see the same kind of grieved anger in yourself? Can you see your face reflected in the face of Jesus?…Note thoughts in your journal.

Read Mark 3:1-6, third reading, followed by reflection and sharing. (15 minutes)

- Before reading the passage once more, invite participants to meditate on the face of hurt and unattended need in the story.

- Read the story again.

- Guide the meditation: **Close your eyes and visualize the man with the withered hand in the presence of the Pharisees.…Step into the man's place and his awareness of what the Pharisees communicate by watching Jesus in silence and refusing to answer him.…As the man, what do you feel toward these religious leaders who would prevent your healing because of Sabbath regulations?…Come back to reflect on your own life. When have you experienced hurt or neglect from people who were just following the rules or enforcing the laws?…**

- In your journal draw a symbolic picture of your "withered hand." It could represent some part of you that is withered by hurt, criticism, or anger and in need of healing; or part of you withered by neglect, a need to be nurtured or to grow in some way. What "withered" part of you needs the life-giving touch of grace? (*Allow a few minutes.*)

- Have group members share briefly what was most meaningful to them from any of these three meditations. Exercise your judgment about whether to share in the whole group or to break into smaller clusters.

CLOSING (10 MINUTES)

If the larger group broke into clusters, regather the group.

Read the following quote by Henri Nouwen:

> When the soil is not plowed the rain cannot reach the seeds; when the leaves are not raked away the sun cannot nurture the hidden plants. So also, when our memories remain covered with fear, anxiety, or suspicion the word of God cannot bear fruit.[1]

Prayerfully review the meeting. Invite the participants to reflect on the gift and challenge of the meeting: **Where has the rain of grace reached your seeds? Where do you sense the leaves not yet raked away?** Allow for brief responses.

Pray for healing and growth. Offer instructions as follows: **Move into a time of quiet prayer with hands opened out. Imagine Jesus turning to you and saying, "Stretch out your hand." Then, if you wish and as you feel ready, silently stretch out your hand (remembering the need it represents as your "withered hand"). Allow the presence of Christ to reach out to you; receive inwardly whatever gift may be given.**

Offer a closing prayer of thanksgiving.

Say a benediction or sing the "Companion Song."

Week 4
Transforming Anger

PREPARATION

Prepare yourself spiritually. Read the article for Week 4, do all the exercises, and keep a journal along with the participants. Given the sensitive nature of the subject matter, be especially diligent in praying for each participant and for your group meeting.

Prepare materials and the meeting space. This week's session requires several items. First, you will need a copy of the "Reflection Sheet on Transforming Anger" for each group member (page 59 of the Leader's Guide). In "Deeper Explorations" you will need a Peace, Hope, and Justice prayer candle as well as one small votive or tea candle for each group member. Please read the section in the "Weekly Needs at a Glance" (pages 5–6) that gives background information about the prayer candle. Be ready to explain briefly to the group the candle's significance. Additionally, you will need hymnals or songbooks. Select songs for the "Opening" and "Closing."

Review the intent of the meeting: that participants get in touch with the power of anger as a force for change when aligned with God's will, and learn practices for turning anger to redemptive ends.

OPENING (10 MINUTES)

Welcome all participants personally as they enter.

Set a context.

This meeting is the fourth of eight sessions exploring *The Way of Forgiveness*. In this meeting we will be sharing our experience with spiritual practices to transform anger.

Join together in worship.

- **We light a candle to remind us of Christ in our midst as we gather in prayer.**

- Read a single verse, John 14:1: **"Do not let your hearts be troubled. Believe in God, believe also in me."**

- Ask members to sit quietly with this verse. Remind them: **Jesus spoke this word of comfort to his disciples, and he speaks it to us as well.**

- After a few minutes of silent reflection, ask some simple questions such as: **What troubles do you carry in your heart? Can you let them go to God? If not, in silent prayer ask the Lord to help you identify what prevents you from doing so.**

- Close with a gentle song such as "O Lord, Hear My Prayer"; "Lead Me, Guide Me"; or "Come and Find the Quiet Center."

SHARING INSIGHTS (45 MINUTES)

During this time, participants will identify and share where they have experienced God's presence in their lives this past week. Begin by reminding group members of this week's theme: transforming anger. The article and the daily exercises have helped them practice different ways of altering their experience of anger through prayerful attention, listening, and giving voice to their feelings.

1. Give participants a few minutes to review the article for this week and their journal entries that accompany the daily exercises.

2. Ask participants to share their insights from the weekly reading and/or from their journal entries. As the leader, model the sharing by offering your brief reflections first. Encourage active and deep listening during this sharing time.

3. Invite participants to pay attention together to the main points or common themes that emerged in this sharing time. What themes were mentioned more than once? Where did participants have similar feelings or experiences? Identify these similarities.

BREAK (10 MINUTES)

DEEPER EXPLORATIONS (45 MINUTES)

Introduce the Peace, Hope, and Justice prayer candle. (3 minutes)

- Give a brief explanation of this candle based on the notes in "Weekly Needs at a Glance" section in the Leader's Guide (pages 5–6). There is also an explanation on page 116 of the Participant's Book.

- Indicate that it will be lit in the "Closing" time.

Set a context. (*2 minutes*) **We are going to explore the story of Jesus' lament over Jerusalem and his transforming anger in the Temple. Here is a little background for our reflection. When Jesus weeps over Jerusalem, he foresees the eventual destruction of the Temple by the Romans. The Temple, a huge complex of buildings, symbolized the religious, political, and economic center of Jewish life. Its destruction involved not only the razing of mammoth structures that had taken decades to build but also the killing and starvation of thousands. The loss of the Temple meant total spiritual and cultural disorientation for the Jewish people.**

Prepare the group to reflect on Luke 19: 41-46 through silence and sharing. (*2 minutes*)

- Encourage group members to have their journals open and be ready to jot down their reflections.

- Invite three volunteers to read this text. Remind them that the first part is a lament.

Read Luke 19:41-46, first reading. (*8 minutes*)

- Invite reading of the Luke passage.

- Ask, **What words describe for you what is going on inside Jesus? What do you perceive his feelings to be in each part of this story—the lament over Jerusalem and cleansing the Temple?**

- Reflect silently.

- Share in the group.

Read Luke 19:41-46, second reading. (*5 minutes*)

- Ask, **If Jesus were physically here among us today, where would he "weep"? Where would he express mourning or outrage? What do you think he would say or do?**

- Reflect silently.

- Share in the group.

Read Luke 19:41-46, third reading, followed by individual exercises and sharing. (25 minutes)

- Before the reading, give each participant a copy of the "Reflection Sheet on Transforming Anger." Note that the phrase *transforming anger* may refer to the way anger, when properly directed, has the power to bring about transformation.

- Invite the third reading of the Luke passage.

- Call group members to a time of personal solitude during which they write their lament and reflect on developing a creative, redemptive response to the situation they have identified.

Work individually. (Allow at least 10 minutes.)

Regather as a total group.

- Invite brief sharing of the laments and the actions chosen. If time permits ask this question: **Is it easier to get in touch with your feelings of mourning or your feelings of outrage?**

Closing (10 minutes)

Arrange smaller votive candles around the larger Peace, Hope, and Justice prayer candle. Have someone light the prayer candle as you read the following.

Read Matthew 5:14-16.

- Follow the reading with these words of a South African Christian: **To light a candle in the darkness is to say, "I beg to differ."**

- Then ask, **In what way is Christ calling you to light a candle in the midst of darkness?**

Invite participants to light a small candle from the larger one. **As you feel led, rise up and light a small candle from the flame of the Peace, Hope, and Justice prayer candle. If you choose, name the situation where you would like to bring light.**

Lead a time of intercessory prayer, inviting people to lift to God the situations that were named.

Sing a song or hymn. Suggestions: "Pass It On" or "Companion Song."

Say or sing a benediction.

Reflection Sheet on Transforming Anger

BASED ON LUKE 19:41-46

As he came near and saw the city, he wept over it....

Name a specific situation where you weep in anguish or outrage with Jesus over the state of God's world.

"If you, even you, had only recognized on this day the things that make for peace! But now they are hidden from your eyes."

Write your lament or mourning directly to God in the form of a prayer, psalm, or letter.

Then he entered the temple and began to drive out those who were selling things there....

Decide to do something creative and redemptive with your anger and grief. Visualize an action you would like to take that would make a positive difference. Describe it in some detail.

Week 5
Receiving God's Forgiveness

PREPARATION

Prepare yourself spiritually. Read the article for Week 5, do all the exercises, and keep a journal along with the participants. Spend time in prayer seeking God's guidance for the group meeting, and pray for each participant.

Prepare materials and the meeting space. The setting for this week's group meeting is the Last Supper. You will need a table large enough to seat all the members of your group, cups with a beverage, paper napkins, and a plate each of bread, cheese, and fruit. Food will be placed on the table at the break. You will also need a small piece of bread reserved for each person. Place the Christ candle on the worship table as usual. Continue use of the Peace, Hope, and Justice prayer candle each week now; position it near the door as a reminder of God's call to be bearers of Christ's light as participants leave. Hymnals or songbooks may also be needed. Find a place in the room to collect or display forgiveness stories that people bring, beginning this week through the end of the course.

Review the intent of this meeting: that participants gain a deeper understanding of what forgiveness is and is not, and a stronger appreciation of our need for God's forgiveness.

OPENING (10 MINUTES)

Welcome all participants personally as they enter. Point out the location for collecting forgiveness stories they may bring.

Set a context.

This is our fifth week together as we journey through *Companions in Christ: The Way of Forgiveness.* This week we are moving toward a fuller understanding of forgiveness, what it is and what it is not. Our particular challenge is to open more fully to God's generous forgiveness of us.

Join together in worship.

- **We light a candle to remind us that Christ is in our midst as we gather.**

- Ask a volunteer to read aloud Psalm 32:1-5. (Consider also reading without discussion a true story of someone *asking for pardon and receiving forgiveness.* This could be a story you bring or one of the stories on pages 89–94 in the appendix of the Leader's Guide.)

- Give everyone a minute in silence to jot down what he or she hears inwardly.

- Take a few minutes to share words, images, or thoughts.

- Close with a song, perhaps "Give Thanks with a Grateful Heart" or one of your favorite hymns of gratitude.

SHARING INSIGHTS (45 MINUTES)

At this point group members will identify their experience of God's presence in their lives this past week. Open this portion of the session by reminding group members of this week's theme: receiving God's forgiveness. The article and the daily exercises have helped them to begin thinking about forgiveness and their need for it.

1. Give participants a few minutes to review the article for this week and their journal entries that accompany the daily exercises.

2. Ask participants to share insights from the weekly reading and/or from their journal entries for the week. As the leader, model the sharing by offering your brief reflections first. Encourage active and deep listening during this sharing time.

3. Ask participants to help you identify the main points or common themes that emerged in this time of sharing. What refrains or echoes were heard?

BREAK (15 MINUTES)

Announce that there will be an extended break with time for some simple food and fellowship. Set out bread, cheese, fruit, and drinks on a table the group can sit around. Allow the sharing of food and fellowship around the table to continue for about five minutes beyond normal break time. Remain at the table for the "Deeper Explorations."

DEEPER EXPLORATIONS (35 MINUTES)

Lay the foundation. (2 minutes)

We have been enjoying ourselves here with good food and fellowship, just like the disciples at table with Jesus. When they gathered for the Last Supper, only Jesus knew it would be the last. As a way to bring into focus our need for forgiveness, we will be meditating in various ways on Mark's account of the Last Supper and events following in the first part of the Passion narrative. The whole text is long, but we will read through it in its entirety only once.

Read Mark 14:17-72. (10 minutes)

- Invite several people to take turns in reading the text. You might begin by reading verses 17-21, then invite others around the circle to read a portion of the story in sequence until the chapter is finished.

- After the reading make several points in your own words: **When Jesus tells the disciples one of them will betray him, they each wonder and worry, "Surely, not I?" The unhappy answer in a deeper sense is "Yes, I." Peter vows never to deny him, yet does so and then weeps bitterly. While only Judas directly betrays Jesus, every disciple deserts him and falls away.**

- Invite reflection with words like these: **Take a minute to ponder the amazing grace in this fact: despite his knowledge that one will betray him, one will deny him, and all will desert him, Jesus stays at the table with them and breaks bread with them, a sign of intimate fellowship. Instead of abandoning his disciples as faithless friends, he responds to their fickleness with forgiveness. He gives his life for them and to them.**

- Ask this question: **What does it mean to you that Jesus stays at the table with these disciples?** (leave several moments for reflection)

- Lead a brief time of sharing. Encourage each person to venture a response to the question.

Read and reflect on verses 17-20 as if a disciple. (8 minutes)

- Ask each person to assume the mind-set of a disciple as you reread a portion of the story.

- Reread verses 17-20.

- Invite self-examination: **Reflect on one way you have in fact denied or deserted Christ or a way you have hurt him by hurting others.…For what attitude or act do you need forgiveness?**

- Allow a time for solitary reflection while still gathered around the table.

- Invite the participants to find a symbolic word or phrase that represents their need of forgiveness (such as "my insensitivity," "Sally," "last August," or "when I lashed out").

- Go around the circle and invite each "disciple" to say his or her symbolic word or phrase.

Read and reflect on verses 22-25 as if you were Jesus. (10 minutes)

- Ask each person to assume the mind of Jesus as you reread another portion of the story.

- Reread verses 22-25.

- Invite participants to look with love, inwardly or outwardly, on the group around the table.

- Ask them then to imagine in their minds and hearts what Jesus would say to them as a group of disciples and to jot it down. (*Give a few minutes for reflection.*)

- Indicate that it is important for us to hear the message of forgiveness from Christ through the faith community. Invite all who wish to share the words of forgiveness and faithfulness they have imagined Jesus might say to the group. Initiate the responses with your own response. Examples might be: "My friends, there is nothing you can do to change my love for you." "Beloved, there is nowhere you can run to escape my love for you." "My children, no matter how great the sin in you, the grace in God will always be greater."

Review the meeting briefly. (5 minutes) **Where was the grace or challenge for you in this time "at the table?" What did you learn?**

CLOSING (15 MINUTES)

Set out a piece of bread for each person around the table.

Sing a song or hymn celebrating God's grace for our need. A Communion hymn would be appropriate, or songs such as "Spirit of the Living God" or "Breathe on Me, Breath of God."

Remind the group that in the Gospel of John, when the risen Christ rejoined the disciples on the evening of his Resurrection day, he gave them (and us) the very power to forgive that God had given him:

> **Jesus said to them again, "Peace be with you. As the Father has sent me, so I send you." When he had said this, he breathed on them and said to them, "Receive the Holy Spirit. If you forgive the sins of any, they are forgiven…"** (John 20:21-23*a*).

Invite participants to pair up around the "supper table." Instruct them to turn to each other and ask, one at a time, "What is your need for forgiveness?" In response, the person asked will briefly name a specific need. The other may then place a hand on the arm or wrist of the person seeking forgiveness and say, "In the name of Jesus Christ, you are forgiven." (As leader, you might briefly model this action with another person while you explain it.) Before proceeding, ask the pairs to take a moment in silent prayer to prepare their hearts for confessing any specific need and for serving as Christ in ministry to their neighbor. Then they may proceed.

Celebrate a modified Love Feast. (See Leader's Note on page 66.)

- Say a few words about the Love Feast, emphasizing that this is not the sacrament of Holy Communion but a related tradition of the church.

- Lift your piece of bread and say words to this effect: **Christ our Lord has given himself to us in forgiving love. Though we fail him time and again, Christ does not fail us. He remains at the table with us as our Lord and Savior. He makes us ministers of grace for one another. As we eat the bread, let's remember God's love with grateful hearts and celebrate the life we share as companions in Christ.**

- Invite all to partake of the bread, to remember and be thankful in silence.

Say or sing a benediction.

Remind participants of the Peace, Hope, and Justice prayer candle near the door and its invitation to bear the light of Christ with them as they leave.

Leader's Note on the Love Feast

This background is provided in case anyone expresses interest in or questions about the nature of the Love Feast that we have modified for the Closing in week 5.

The Love Feast, or Agape Meal, is a Christian fellowship meal recalling the meals Jesus shared with disciples during his ministry and expressing the fellowship of forgiveness and grace enjoyed by the family of Christ.

Although its early origins are closely connected with the Lord's Supper, the two services became quite distinct and should not be confused with each other. The modern history of the Love Feast began when Moravians in Germany introduced it in the eighteenth century as a service of sharing food, prayer, religious conversation, and hymns. When John Wesley picked up the practice and made it part of his ministry, it became a regular feature of the evangelical revival and of Methodist society meetings.

The Love Feast has often been held on occasions when the celebration of the Lord's Supper would be inappropriate or difficult: when no one present is authorized to administer the sacrament, when persons of different denominations are present who do not feel free to take Holy Communion together, when there is a desire for a service more informal and spontaneous than the Communion ritual, or at a full meal or some other setting to which it would be difficult to adapt the Lord's Supper. One of the advantages of the Love Feast is that any Christian may conduct it.

Most Love Feasts include the sharing of food such as ordinary bread, crackers, rolls, or sweet bread baked especially for this service. It is customary not to use Communion bread, wine, or grape juice because to do so might confuse the Love Feast with the Lord's Supper. The beverage has usually been water, but other beverages such as lemonade, tea, or coffee have been used. When the Love Feast is shared in the course of a full meal, leftover food may be taken to persons not present as an expression of love.

Background and orders for the Love Feast can be found in various denominational worship materials.

Adapted from "Occasional Services," *The United Methodist Book of Worship* (Nashville, Tenn.: The United Methodist Publishing House, 1992), 581–82.

Week 6
Forgiving Others

PREPARATION

Prepare yourself spiritually. Read the article for Week 6, do all the exercises, and keep your own journal. Spend time in prayer for your next group meeting and for each group member, including you, to be open to discover the way of forgiveness.

Prepare materials and the meeting space. Prepare to teach the Lord's Prayer with a few simple movements for the "Opening" (pages 72–73). Make copies of the "Reflection Sheet on Your Debtor's Prison" (page 74) for each group member. You will need a large pottery or glass bowl filled with water and a half-inch layer of sand in the bottom, along with another container filled with plenty of small, smooth stones. ("River rocks" can be purchased by the bag at Pier 1 Imports.) Plan to keep these items handy for the remaining group meetings. You will also need the Peace, Hope, and Justice prayer candle. Secure hymnals or songbooks, and set up room space as usual.

Review the intent of this meeting: that group members will gain a deeper openness to forgiveness and a greater willingness to extend it to others as God has extended it to them.

OPENING (10 MINUTES)

Welcome participants with a personal greeting as they enter.

Set a context.

This is the sixth week on our journey through *Companions in Christ: The Way of Forgiveness.* Last week we looked at the depth of our need to be forgiven. This week we are exploring our equally profound need to forgive others.

Join together in worship.

- **We light a candle to represent Christ, who stands in our midst longing to give us his own compassionate heart and generous spirit.**

- Deuteronomy 15:1-2 introduces God's command to Israel to cancel debts every seven years. Read the passage aloud. Invite group members to ponder and discuss briefly what it would be like suddenly to discover that all their financial debts were canceled—marked "paid in full"—with no strings or obligations.

- In closing ask the group to consider silently what debts they have held against others for long periods of time. What would it take for them to release one of those debts and mark it "paid in full"?

- Close by leading the group through the Lord's Prayer with simple hand movements. (See pages 72–73.)

SHARING INSIGHTS (45 MINUTES)

At this time group members identify and share where they have experienced God's presence in their lives this past week. Begin by reminding group members of the theme for this week: forgiving others. The article and the daily exercises for this week have helped participants begin the inner work that may lead to offering forgiveness freely.

1. Allow a brief time for participants to review the article for this week as well as their journal entries that accompany the daily exercises.

2. Ask participants to share their insights from the weekly reading and/or from their journal entries. As the leader, model the sharing by offering your brief reflections first. Encourage active and deep listening during this sharing time.

3. Invite the group to identify the main points or common themes that have surfaced. What patterns emerged in the sharing time?

BREAK (10 MINUTES)

Deeper Explorations (40 minutes)

Set a context. (3 minutes)

Read Matthew 18:21-22. This brief exchange between Peter and Jesus sets the stage for one of Jesus' most convicting parables, the parable of the unforgiving servant. Jesus reminds Peter that forgiveness is not a matter of arithmetic, and the parable effectively makes the case that our unwillingness to forgive one another resembles the behavior of the first slave in this story. Our own forgiveness is directly related to our ability to forgive. Here is the challenge we are called to explore as we meditate on this parable.

Read Matthew 18:23-33, first reading. (5 minutes)

- Read the full text without rushing.

- Invite participants into a time of silent reflection as they get in touch with their own images of debt and credit—financial, emotional, legal. **What are the realities of debt and credit in our culture and in our personal lives? How do these realities connect to our relationship with God?** (Jot down your thoughts.)

- Share briefly around the circle images of debt and credit.

Read Matthew 18:23-27, second reading. (5 minutes)

- Ask, **When have you felt like the first slave, knowing that you owe God everything you are and have, yet that you are forgiven?** Invite silent reflection.

- Share briefly around the circle.

Read Matthew 18:28-33, third reading. (5 minutes)

- Ask, Whom have we thrown into our debtor's prisons? Every one of us has a dungeon inside where we hold captive those who owe us for aggravation, insult, cheating, lying, manipulation, or any form of harm. Since we began our list in daily exercise 1, who is still in our dungeon? Are there any we want to add? We will know they are there if we go in every so often and "beat them up" with angry thoughts, vengeful fantasies, bad wishes and curses, and resentful replays of conversations in which we really "tell them off." We will also know they are there if we are still treating them differently now (avoidance, sniping remarks, emotional distance, and so on).

Solitary reflection on the image of debtor's prison. (*10 minutes*)

- Encourage each participant to find some personal space.

- Hand out the "Reflection Sheet on Your Debtor's Prison."

- Indicate that you will ring a bell or call out at the end of 10 minutes, a signal for them to return to the group.

Invite participants to share what they have discovered for themselves. (*12 minutes*) Guide conversation with these questions:

- **What does your prison look or feel like (images, symbols, characteristics, feelings)?**

- **What is your "cost/benefit" analysis of maintaining it?**

- **What would it look or feel like to set your prisoners free?**

CLOSING (15 MINUTES)

Set out symbols. On the center worship table set a bowl filled with water and some sand in the bottom. Set beside it the container filled with stones. (You might want to scatter stones around the bowl as well.) Light the Peace, Hope, and Justice prayer candle.

Sing a song or hymn related to the theme of mercy such as "There's a Wideness in God's Mercy."

Offer a ritual to indicate forgiveness.

- Sound the call to forgive as we have been forgiven by reading the following quote from Abbé de Tourville:

  Do not keep accounts with our Lord….Go bankrupt! Let our Lord love you without justice! Say frankly, "He loves me because I do not deserve it…that is why I, in my turn, love Him as well as I can."…Therefore burn your account books![1]

- "Burn your account books!" These words challenge us not merely to release prisoners one by one but to close down our dungeon altogether.

- Explain the symbols on the table. **We may think of Jesus' words, "Let anyone among you who is without sin be the first to throw a stone." These stones could serve as reminders of our hard judgments, but in letting go of them we use them to express our forgiveness of others.** Indicate that the bowl with water and sand represents the depths of the sea. Starting now and through the end of the weekly meetings, whenever participants in the group feel they have made real progress, taken some action, or found inner movement toward releasing someone from their prison, they may take a stone and drop it into the depths of the sea. They may also "name" the stone, or drop it in silence.

- The group will respond to any members who choose to drop in stones by saying, "Blessed are the merciful, for they will receive mercy!" Demonstrate this by dropping a stone in the water and letting the group practice the response.

- Assure participants that it is okay if they do not yet feel ready for this gesture. Perhaps they will be ready next week or the following week. Then invite any who feel ready for this symbolic act to follow you.

Invite prayers of thanksgiving and intercession.

Say or sing a benediction such as "God Be with You Till We Meet Again."

The Lord's Prayer with Movements

Invite members to find a partner and stand facing each other. If you have an uneven number in your group, make groups of three as needed. Begin by teaching the movements without any connection to words. This will help your participants learn the movements more quickly.

Movements:

- Start with arms bent in front of you, palms facing up.
- Place the hands on the chest over the heart.
- Extend the arms in an upward diagonal direction, meeting your partner's hands high—like London Bridge.
- Reach up, separating one pair of hands.
- Reach up, separating the other pair of hands.
- Bring your hands down and look to the earth.
- Reach up with your hands, not touching your partner.
- Cup your two hands together in front of you as if receiving something.
- Make a fist and press your knuckles against your partner's knuckles.
- Unclench your fists and link fingers, holding hands with your partner in front of you.
- Continue to hold hands; turn your left hands upside-down to reveal your wrists.
- Repeat the same motion as above but with other hands.
- Shake your right hands as in a handshake…and don't let go.
- Shake left hands as in a handshake. Now you have both hands clasped.
- Let go of each other's hands and make twinkle stars with your fingers.
- Form your hands in a prayer fashion and bow slightly to partner.

Repeat the actions with your group.

Now add the words to the movements:

Our Father…(or other name for God)

- Start with arms bent in front of you, palms facing up.

who art in Heaven…

- Place the hands on the chest over the heart.

hallowed be thy name…

- Extend the arms in an upward diagonal direction, meeting your partner's hands high—like London Bridge.

Thy kingdom come…

- Reach up, separating one pair of hands.

Thy will be done…

- Reach up, separating the other pair of hands.

on earth…

- Bring your hands down and look to the earth.

as it is in heaven.

- Reach up with your hands, not touching your partner.

Give us this day our daily bread…

- Cup your two hands together in front of you as if receiving something.

and forgive us our debts…

- Make a fist and press your knuckles against your partner's knuckles.

as we forgive our debtors…

- Unclench your fists and link fingers, holding hands with your partner in front of you.

And lead us not into temptation…

- Continue to hold hands; turn your left hands upside-down to reveal your wrists.

but deliver us from evil…

- Repeat the same motion as above but with your other hands.

For thine is the kingdom…

- Shake your right hands as in a handshake…and don't let go.

and the power…

- Shake your left hands as in a handshake. Now you have both hands clasped.

and the glory forever…

- Let go of each other's hands and make twinkle stars with your fingers.

Amen.

- Form your hands in a prayer fashion and bow slightly to your partner.

From *The Worship Workbook* by Marcia McFee © 2002 by Abingdon Press. Adapted and reprinted by permission.

Reflection Sheet on Your Debtor's Prison

Whom have you thrown into your debtor's prison? Review your journal response to exercise 1 from this past week. Are there any names you need to add? You may wish to record only first names, initials, or symbols for the persons you list.

Draw an image or symbol of the prison(s) you maintain. Your prison may be a heavily defended place with strong doors and bars. It may be carefully disguised with shrubs and flowers so no one suspects its function. It could be a place of deep pain—a broken heart or home, a wrecked car, a divorce decree. Let your feelings and imagination help you find an image (or more than one) that fits your experience.

Consider what it costs you to maintain this prison, the price you pay in your body, mind, energy, spirit, and relationships. Reflect too on what you gain from maintaining it.

Now simply sit in your prison with this portion of the Lord's Prayer:

Forgive us our debts as we forgive our debtors.

What would it be like to release all these prisoners, to forgive their debts and set them free? What would it feel like to come back tomorrow and find the dungeon empty?

Week 7
Seeking Reconciliation

PREPARATION

Prepare yourself spiritually. Read the article for Week 7, do all the exercises, and keep your own journal. As group members struggle with the challenges of forgiveness and reconciliation, pray that God will prepare you and each participant to receive the greatest benefit from the group meeting.

Prepare materials and the meeting space. Select songs and gather hymnals or songbooks. Arrange the room with a center table and Christ candle. Locate a few pictures of the World Trade Center attacks (from old newspapers or magazines or from the Internet). You will also need more recent newspapers and magazines, and several pairs of scissors. Remember to keep the Peace, Hope, and Justice prayer candle on the worship table and to have the bowl of water and container of stones in an accessible place. Designate the location in your meeting room for collecting and displaying stories of forgiveness and reconciliation.

Review the intent of this meeting: that participants will deepen their understanding of, and willingness to enter into, reconciling forgiveness.

OPENING (10 MINUTES)

Welcome all participants warmly as they enter. Invite participants to place any stories they have brought in the area you have designated for display.

Set a context.

This meeting is the seventh on our deepening journey into the life of forgiveness and reconciliation. This week we are exploring what it means to seek reconciliation in broken relationships.

Remind participants that any time they feel they have taken a step toward forgiveness or reconciliation, they may drop a stone into the "sea" (with no need for explanation). The group need not interrupt what they are doing to respond, but members may wish to offer a personal word of encouragement or celebration to one another at appropriate times.

Join together in worship.

- **We light a candle to remember that Christ is in our midst as we gather. May the light of Christ illumine our path toward accepting and extending the precious gift of forgiveness.**

- Read 2 Corinthians 5:17-20.

- Ask members to consider silently if they are serving as God's ambassadors for reconciliation in the world. As they review each of the many environments in which they live (home, church, work, community, world), encourage them to identify one setting in which they respond to God's call to be in an active ministry of reconciliation.

- Offer a brief prayer expressing gratitude that God has not held our trespasses against us but has entrusted us with the message of reconciliation. Give members an opportunity to voice thanks by naming an area of their lives where they have experienced being reconciled or are able to act as reconcilers.

- Close by singing "Give Thanks with a Grateful Heart"; "Freely, Freely," or another favorite hymn.

SHARING INSIGHTS (45 MINUTES)

For the next 45 minutes, group members will have an opportunity to identify and share where they have experienced God's presence in their lives this past week. Begin by reminding group members of the theme for this week: seeking reconciliation. The article for this week introduces the idea of reconciliation and explores how it relates to forgiveness. The daily exercises help group members see how forgiveness and reconciliation can be practiced in their own lives.

1. Ask participants to take a few minutes to look over the article for the week as well as their journal entries based on the daily exercises.

2. Invite participants to share their insights from the weekly reading and/or from their journal entries for the week. As the leader, model the sharing by offering your brief reflections first. Encourage active and deep listening during this sharing time.

3. Encourage the group to identify the main points or common themes that have emerged. What patterns seem to be surfacing in the sharing time?

Break (10 minutes)

Deeper Explorations (45 minutes)

Set a context. (10 minutes)

- The great twentieth-century theologian H. Richard Niebuhr spoke of the church as a "social pioneer." In Niebuhr's understanding the church is called to be the first to repent, the first to forgive, the first to build bridges between peoples locked in fruitless conflict. Everywhere we look in this world, we see abundant evidence of the need for reconciliation. As followers of Christ we have many opportunities to be social and spiritual pioneers.

- Name a few of the most recent expressions of division and conflict nationally and globally. Then focus on the World Trade Center attack, using one or more pictures to remind the group of its emotional impact and deep wounding of one nation's psyche. Take several minutes to explore the question, Who are our enemies?

Meditate on the Parable of the Good Samaritan. (15 minutes)

We are going to let the parable of the Good Samaritan focus our reflections. This story is so familiar that we tend to think of it as encouragement to do a good daily deed. But if we understand the social context, we can see that both forgiveness and reconciliation are implied in this parable. The Samaritans were considered by the Jews to be a "bastard" people, a mixed breed who had common ancestors with the Jews but who had intermarried with Gentiles and lost the purity of Jewish faith in the process. Therefore the Jews considered Samaritans unclean. They refused to use any eating or drinking utensils in common with Samaritans for fear of defilement. Samaritans were despised, avoided, and persecuted by Jews. The Samaritans in turn despised the Jews. For Jesus to tell this parable in a way that forces the Jewish lawyer to call the Samaritan "neighbor" is in itself a radical call to reconciliation.

- *Read Luke 10:25-37.* After a few moments of reflection, invite participants to name in a word or phrase what they see, hear, and feel in the interaction of these characters.

- *Read Luke 10:25-37 again.* Ask the following questions with a minute or so of silence for reflection and journaling after each one.

  1. The Samaritan "was moved with pity." Given the history of hurt between Samaritans and Jews, what immediate thoughts or feelings might he have had to overcome in order to act with compassion?

  2. Imagine how the innkeeper might respond. Suppose he were a Jew....Suppose he were a Samaritan....

  3. In your life who are the "Samaritans" and "Jews"? What are the cultural, political, economic, or ethnic divides that affect you? Do you feel a real sense of enmity with some of these people?

Lead an exercise on identifying our enemies. (10 minutes)

- Spread out several recent newspapers and news magazines along with several pairs of scissors.

- Come back to the question, Who are our enemies? Invite participants to take a newspaper or magazine and look for pictures or headlines that represent in some way their response to question 3 (above). Ask them to tear or quickly cut these out and place them on the floor or table between them. (*5 minutes*)

- Invite group members to respond to what they see here. Look together at the images and comment or ask questions as you are moved.

Lead a guided prayer for our enemies. (10 minutes)

- Look at these pictures. Which of these images represents an enemy you would feel challenged to pray for?

- Imagine that you are going along one day when you suddenly see an enemy lying in the street or hallway, badly wounded. Get in touch with who you see...(It might be an image from among those we have collected, or a more personal image.) Now get in touch with your immediate response...

- Envision Jesus standing beside you saying, "Love your enemies and pray for those who persecute you."... Allow the compassion of Christ to surface and grow warm in you.... Offer a prayer of blessing if you feel empowered by God's spirit to do so....

- Invite participants to reflect on the experience. Where did they find grace or challenge in this process?

CLOSING (10 MINUTES)

Light the Peace, Hope, and Justice prayer candle.

Read Romans 12:9-21, followed by a time of silent reflection.

Sing a song or hymn with a theme of unity and reconciliation such as "They'll Know We Are Christians by Our Love."

Guide the group in a litany of intercessory prayer for enemies.

> Each person lifts up one name or image that arose from the guided prayer experience, saying, "For _____, in peace let us pray to the Lord."
>
> The group responds by saying, "Lord, have mercy."
>
> Conclude by singing a hymn verse or chant such as "Jesus, Remember Me."

Say a benediction.

Becoming the Beloved Community

PREPARATION

Prepare yourself spiritually. Read the article for Week 8. Do all the exercises and keep a journal along with the participants. This will be the concluding meeting related to this resource for your group. Pray for each participant and for your leadership, that you may perceive clearly what God calls forth from you as a result of this time together.

Prepare materials and the meeting space. Make sure you have hymnals or songbooks and select a song for the "Opening" and "Closing." Arrange the room with a center table and the Christ candle. Place on the table a small cross for each group member, and a small bowl with oil. Position the Peace, Hope, and Justice prayer candle near the door as a reminder of our call to be bearers of light in the midst of darkness. Write the opening responsive sentences for the "Closing" on newsprint (page 85). Prepare a place to continue collecting or displaying stories of forgiveness and reconciliation.

Review the intent of this meeting: that participants review together the spiritual fruit of these eight weeks, and discern first steps in their call to participate in the ongoing mission of God's reconciling love in this world.

OPENING (10 MINUTES)

Welcome all participants personally as they enter. Invite them to place or post their forgiveness stories in the designated area.

Set a context.

This is the final meeting on our journey through *The Way of Forgiveness*. In this session we come full circle, back to the place where God's generous grace enfolds us both as individuals and as a community. As we conclude these eight weeks together, we will give special consideration to how we take what we've received back to our church and community.

Join together in worship.

- Begin by lighting the candle, a reminder of God's faithful presence in your midst from the beginning of your time together.

- Read Colossians 3:12-15.

- Invite the group to repeat the words and phrases that are especially rich for them.

- Remain for a few minutes in quiet contemplation of the verses people lift up. Punctuate the silence with a rereading of select phrases such as "Let the peace of Christ rule in your hearts."

- Close by singing "Let There Be Peace on Earth" or a similar song of your choice.

SHARING INSIGHTS (45 MINUTES)

During this time participants will identify and share where they have experienced God's presence in their lives this past week. Begin by reminding group members of the theme for this week: becoming "the beloved community." The article and daily exercises explore forgiveness and reconciliation in our wider communities.

1. Give participants a few minutes to review the article for this week and their journal entries that accompany the daily exercises.

2. Ask participants to share insights from the weekly reading and/or from their journal entries for the week. As the leader, model the sharing by offering your brief reflections first. Encourage active and deep listening during this sharing time.

3. Bring out the main points or common themes that have emerged in the sharing time. What themes were mentioned more than once? Where did participants have similar feelings or experiences? Is there a "word" from God in these common threads?

BREAK (10 MINUTES)

DEEPER EXPLORATIONS (45 MINUTES)

Explore God's call to be ambassadors of Christ with a ministry of reconciliation.

Set a context. (2 minutes)

> The last paragraph of our article for this week begins with these words: "In the final analysis, forgiveness can only emerge from great strength of soul. It is a clear sign of the courageous, humble resilience of the human spirit undergirded by grace" (page 99, Participant's Book).
>
> Indicate that the group will use its final hour to do two things:
>
> 1) review what you have received during your journey together that has contributed to your capacity to forgive, your strength of soul;
>
> 2) listen to where God is calling you to exercise the ministry of reconciliation that has been given you.

Review the gifts you have received. (8 minutes)

• Ask participants, **What is the most valuable thing you have learned or received during these eight weeks that has contributed to the "strength of soul" in you that is required to forgive?**

• Allow a minute of quiet reflection.

• Invite each participant to share one response.

Listen for Christ's call. (15 minutes)

• Read the story of Elias Chacour (page 86)—an example of how one person heard the call to a ministry of reconciliation in the midst of a highly conflicted situation. Allow a few moments for the group to absorb the story.

• Ask someone to read 2 Corinthians 5:16-21. Return to a focus on the first half of verse 20: "**So we are ambassadors for Christ, since God is making his appeal through us....**" By "us," Paul meant not only individual members of the Christian community but also the community as a whole, the body of Christ.

• Ask the group, **To whom does God want to appeal through us—not just as individuals but perhaps as a group, a group that has traveled the way of forgiveness together? What would be the nature of that appeal?**

- Invite participants to several minutes of quiet to meditate on the idea that God is appealing for reconciliation through them. Encourage them to focus their minds and open their hearts in listening for God's call—through their memory of this week's daily exercises, the time of sharing insights, and the inspiration of the Holy Spirit. What concerns for reconciliation surface that are compelling, persistent, and too big to respond to alone?

Share the sense of call. (20 minutes)

- Invite participants to share around the circle what they heard during their quiet time.

- As each person shares, encourage the group to listen for God's call to the "body of Christ" represented in this group.

- Ask participants to name and celebrate where they are hearing the call of God, and to identify what they want to do about it.

- If possible, help the group develop a plan of action in response to a common sense of calling or to acknowledge the obstacles to their taking an action. (See the Leader's Notes on "Ideas for Active Response to the Call" on page 87.)

CLOSING (10 MINUTES)

Place small crosses and a bowl of oil on the worship table. Post the responsive sentences written on newsprint for all to see.

Sing "Here I Am, Lord" or another song of self-offering.

Explain the purpose and symbols of this final "Closing."

- The purpose of this closing time is to claim the grace of the Holy Spirit and to be sent forth to respond to God's call.

- The crosses represent God's appeal to us in Christ to be reconciled, then to take up the cross and follow Jesus' ongoing ministry of reconciliation in this world.

- The anointing oil represents God's healing presence and power for ministry. Oil is an ancient Christian symbol of the seal and gifts of the Holy Spirit.

Offer instructions as follows:

After we read the opening sentences, you will have a chance to come forward and "take up a cross" if you feel ready to participate in Jesus' ministry of reconciliation. Whether

or not you feel ready for such a ministry, you are welcome to receive anointing with oil—a symbol of healing for us all, and a sign of the empowerment of the Holy Spirit for those who commit to following the way of Christ.

Lead the opening responsive sentences:

Leader: God reconciled us to himself through Christ;

Group: And God gives us the ministry of reconciliation.

Invite participants to come forward to take a cross, if they are willing, and to receive anointing with oil. Anoint the palm of each person's hand with a personal blessing, adjusting the words based on whether or not the person chose to take up a cross.

Examples:

(Name), may God bless you with fullness of healing and renewed strength for the journey into forgiveness and reconciliation.

(Name), may God bless you with all courage and spiritual power to follow in the way of Jesus' reconciling ministry.

Lead a brief time of thankful prayer.

Offer a closing benediction or sing the "Companion Song."

Remind participants of the Peace, Hope, and Justice prayer candle near the door and its invitation to bear the light of Christ with them as they leave.

A Story of Forgiveness

A Palestinian Israeli Christian pastor, Elias Chacour had recently become priest of the congregation in Ibillin, Israel. The village was bitterly divided in many ways by the intractable conflicts of this region. Within some families, blood brothers would not speak to each other even after their mother's death. When Chacour tried unsuccessfully to preach ecumenism, he received a note from a parishioner: "Begin first to reconcile brothers, sisters, families together." The priest was stung by the truth of those words.

On Palm Sunday, 1966, he preached an uninspired sermon to a crowd in which personal enemies sat far from each other with no eye contact. He felt deeply burdened because the words of the liturgy about the peace of Christ were so far from the reality in their midst. At the end of the service, he felt compelled to act. He strode down the aisle, locked the only doors to the church, and took the key. Chacour then told his people he was grieved at their hatred and maliciousness toward each other. He wondered what the Muslim community must think about their divisiveness. He said he had tried to unite them and failed. Then he said,

> "This morning while I celebrated the liturgy, I found someone who is able to help you. In fact, he is the only one who can work the miracle of reconciliation in this village. This person who can reconcile you is Jesus Christ, and he is here with us.…
>
> "So on Christ's behalf, I say this to you: The doors of the church are locked. Either you kill each other right here in your hatred and then I will celebrate your funerals gratis, or you use this opportunity to be reconciled together before I open the doors of the church."

Tense silence inched by for ten minutes. Finally, a man stood up. It was the village policeman, dressed in his uniform. He stretched out his arms and said, "I ask forgiveness of everybody here and I forgive everybody. And I ask God to forgive me my sins." The man embraced Chacour, then his brothers. Tears flowed, and words of confession and forgiveness passed between people who had not spoken to each other for years. The peace of Christ became real. This dead congregation experienced the resurrection a week before Easter.

Adapted from Elias Chacour with Mary E. Jensen, *We Belong to the Land: The Story of a Palestinian Israeli Who Lives for Peace and Reconciliation* (San Francisco: HarperSanFranciso, 1990), 30–31.

Leader's Notes:
Ideas for Active Response to the Call

The Way of Forgiveness ends by inviting your group to choose a concrete action to carry out after the eight-week resource has been completed. The purpose of such an action is to ensure that the community or church receives a blessing from the presence of a *Way of Forgiveness* group in its midst. An active response also helps to counteract the notion that forgiveness is something we express only inwardly or individually. Forgiveness is a sacred gift and ministry for which we share responsibility as Christians and with which God can change the world.

To stimulate your mind as a group leader, here are some starter ideas for responsive action. Whatever action a group chooses should arise from its own listening process and be relevant in its local setting.

- Hold a "banquet." Choose a response to daily exercise 2 in Week 8 (page 100, Participant's Book). Then decide what do to afterward to validate the gesture as a sign of desired reconciliation.

- Schedule a special time in worship to share testimonies and forgiveness stories with the congregation.

- Confess corporate sin and ask forgiveness of some person or group whose relationship to the community remains wounded by a history of hurt.

- Reach out in an act of fellowship that builds bridges where walls have previously divided. Choose a response to daily exercise 3 in Week 8 (page 101, Participant's Book).

- Extend a hand of friendship to other religious groups, especially those that are rejected, feared, or stereotyped (e.g., Muslims, Jews, Fundamentalists).

- Reach out in an act of fellowship to those who are different, such as kids who "act out," teens who dress oddly, mentally or physically disabled persons.

Appendix
Stories of Forgiveness and Reconciliation

HELA EHRLICH

Hela Ehrlich lost all her grandparents and childhood friends in the Holocaust. Over time her pain turned into a deep bitterness with which she struggled daily. She wanted to forgive but found her heart hard. One day she saw that she could never forgive the Nazis until she recognized their humanity, even in their guilt.

> Trembling, I realized that if I looked into my own heart I could find seeds of hatred there, too. Arrogant thoughts, feelings of irritation toward others, coldness, anger, envy, and indifference—these are the roots of what happened in Nazi Germany. And they are there in *every* human being.
>
> As I recognized—more clearly than ever before—that I myself stood in desperate need of forgiveness, I was able to forgive, and finally I felt completely free.

Johann Christoph Arnold, *Why Forgive?* (Farmington, Pa.: The Plough Publishing House, 2000), 18–19.

JOSEF BEN-ELIEZER

Josef Ben-Eliezer, the son of Polish Jews, experienced forcible expulsion along with other Jews from the town in which his family lived. They were given only a few hours' notice. The Germans force-marched them all to a desolate area, beating some and stripping everyone they searched of their valuables. Many years later Josef escaped to Palestine and saw the birth of the state of Israel. Determined not to let anyone trample him again, he joined the army to fight "the Arabs, who wanted 'our' land." Then one day he found himself forcing Palestinian villagers out of their homes within hours.

> We didn't allow them to leave in peace, but turned on them out of sheer hatred. While interrogating them, we beat them brutally and even murdered some of them. We had not been ordered to do this but acted on our own initiative. Our lowest instincts had been released.

Suddenly, my childhood in wartime Poland flashed before my eyes....Here, too, were people—men, women, and children—fleeing with whatever they could carry. And there was fear in their eyes, a fear that I myself knew all too well.

After great distress, disillusionment, and searching, Josef discovered another Jew—Jesus—"someone who has very little to do with all the violence that is carried out in his name." He realized that Jesus desired to gather all people together across nations, races, and religions, and that this meant "the healing of hatred, and the forgiveness of sins." In his new faith he has experienced the reality of forgiveness and asks himself, "How, then, can you not forgive others?"

Arnold, 19–23.

BILL CHADWICK

Bill Chadwick lost his son Michael to a drunk driver and was determined to get justice. Yet even after the young driver received a sentence, Bill felt no "closure." He felt only "a big hole in my soul." He finally realized he would not find closure without forgiveness.

No amount of punishment could ever even the score. I had to be willing to forgive without the score being even....The road to forgiveness was long and painful....I had to forgive Michael, and God (for allowing it to happen), and myself. Ultimately, it was forgiving myself that was the most difficult. There were many times in my own life I had driven Michael places when I myself was under the influence of alcohol. ...My anger at other people was just my own fear turned outward. I had projected my own guilt onto others ... so that I would not have to look at myself. And it wasn't until I could see my part in this that my outlook could change.

This is what I learned: that the closure we seek comes in forgiving. And this closure is really up to us, because the power to forgive does not lie outside us, but within.

Arnold, 48–50.

GHAIDAA

Ghaidaa lost nine children in the destruction of Al Amariyah, a massive, reinforced concrete shelter in Baghdad that was penetrated by American "smart bombs" during the Gulf War.

More than one thousand Iraqi civilians were incinerated in the bombing, most of them women and children.

Today, Ghaidaa leads tourists among the shelter ruins, hoping that those who see its horrors…will speak out against future bombings. After taking one of Ghaidaa's tours, Carroll and Doris [an American couple], stunned, asked her to forgive them for what America had done to her family and people. A former Air Force officer who had flown bombing sorties over Europe in World War II, Carroll especially felt he bore a share of the guilt. Shaking his hand, then hugging Doris and bursting into tears, Ghaidaa cried, "I forgive you."

Ghaidaa will never find "justice" on human terms. How can one ever replace nine dead children? She will certainly never be able to forget them. But in finding the hearts of two people who asked her to forgive them, she has found something much greater.

Arnold, 52.

CHRIS CARRIER

Chris Carrier was only ten years old when one of his father's recently fired employees abducted, tortured, and tried to kill him. Miraculously Chris survived this vicious attack, but for years he suffered from intense anxiety and unhappiness. At thirteen he realized that he could be much worse off and that his anger would change nothing. "He decided to stop feeling sorry for himself, and to get on with his life instead." Later Chris was informed of his abductor's whereabouts and chose to visit him. The man was old, blind, and ruined from alcohol and smoking. The man expressed his remorse for what he had done to Chris as a boy, and Chris, looking at him, could feel nothing but compassion. They developed a friendship before the man's death. Few people understood Chris's ability to forgive his abductor, but Chris was clear about why he did:

> There is a very pragmatic reason for forgiving. When we are wronged, we can either respond by seeking revenge, or we can forgive. If we choose revenge, our lives will be consumed by anger. When vengeance is served, it leaves one empty. Anger is a hard urge to satisfy and can become habitual. But forgiveness allows us to move on.
>
> There is also a more compelling reason to forgive. Forgiveness is a gift—it is mercy. It is a gift that I have received and also given away. In both cases, it has been completely satisfying.

Arnold, 54–59.

KATE

Kate's father worked twelve-hour days and was rarely at home. Her mother began drinking and neglecting her children. Kate, the oldest of five, struggled to care for younger siblings from the time she was thirteen years old. Things went from bad to worse. Kate discovered her parents had been forced to marry because her mother was already carrying her. Beyond blaming Kate for everything, her mother sometimes became physically abusive in her drunkenness. When sober, she denied all responsibility for harming her daughter.

Kate married young and tried to forget about her mother. But several years later, after the birth of one of her children, Kate's husband urged her to be reconciled with her mother. By now her mother had stopped drinking and wanted to reestablish contact. Kate talked to their pastor, hoping he would assure her that she was fully justified in refusing to allow her mother back into her life.

> All he said was, "You have to come to peace with your mother."
> I said, "You don't know my mother."
> He replied, "That has nothing to do with it."

Her mother did visit, and Kate did not make it easy for her. But in the last few days of the visit, she sensed that her mother was trying to tell her something.

> She even seemed willing to listen to what I had to say to her. As we talked, I realized that Mother wanted a new relationship (by then I desperately wanted one, too) and that she was determined to remove whatever was in the way. It was then that I knew I had to forgive her, so I did. Immediately a wave of relief and healing came over me. It was indescribable, and it has stayed with me to this day.

Arnold, 107–111.

KEFA SEMPANGI

It was Easter morning at the Redeemed Church in Kampala, Uganda. The service, with 7,000 faithful from every walk of life and as far as eighty miles away, had just ended. Pastor Kefa Sempangi was exhausted but joyful. He pushed through the crowds toward the vestry, where he hoped for a few minutes of quiet prayer. Five men followed him in, escaping his notice until they shut the door behind him. He turned and recognized the tribal scars of Idi Amin's notorious Nubian assassins.

The tallest spoke: "We are going to kill you. If you have something to say, say it before you die." His face was twisted with hate.

Sempangi stared at him, feeling the sickening weight of his rage. His mouth felt heavy and his limbs began to shake. He thought, "They will not need to kill me. I am just going to fall over. I am going to fall over dead and I will never see my family again."

As he was thinking what would become of his wife and child, he heard a voice from far away and was astonished to realize it was his own. "I am a dead man already," he heard himself say. "My life is dead and hidden in Christ. It is your lives that are in danger, you are dead in your sins. I will pray to God that after you have killed me, He will spare you from eternal destruction."

In an instant the tall man's face had changed from hatred to curiosity. He lowered his gun and signaled the others to do the same. "Will you pray for us now?" he asked.

"Yes, I will pray for you," the pastor answered. "Please bow your heads and close your eyes." The men obeyed at a signal from their leader, but Sempangi kept his eyes open thinking the request was a trick. Still he prayed: "Father in heaven, you who have forgiven men in the past, forgive these men also. Do not let them perish in their sins but bring them into yourself."

Sempangi admits it was a simple prayer prayed in deep fear. Yet God honored the prayer, for when the men raised their heads their faces had changed. The leader spoke first: "You have helped us, and we will help you….Do not fear for your life. It is in our hands and you will be protected."

Later these men began attending Sempangi's church, using their positions to help church members whose lives were in danger and even helping some to escape from Uganda.

Abridged from Kefa Sempangi, "Easter Morning," *Weavings* 3, no. 3 (May/June 1988): 33-36, originally excerpted from Kefa Sempangi, *A Distant Grief* (Glendale, Calif.: Regal, 1979), 115–121.

A Parable (a fictional account by L. William Countryman)

THE TWO DEBTORS

Two accountants worked for the same, very rich employer, and each of them independently used some of their employer's funds to speculate in securities. They didn't intend to steal the money, they just believed that they were very good at investments, and they expected to present their employer with a handsome profit by and by and to get praised for their good work. Instead, in the same market crash they both lost everything they had staked.

Both of them ran away. But they were people of principle, and they were very distressed by the way things had turned out. Each of them separately resolved to devote his life to replacing what he had wasted.

Through austerity, self-denial, and better investing, each of them finally succeeded in accumulating the needed amount. By chance, they returned on the same day, which happened to be their employer's birthday.

The first came in, made himself known, and explained that he was there to repay the money he had lost all those years before. But when the employer recognized him, he exclaimed, "Oh, that's right! That's who you are. But I can't accept the money. I forgave the debt years ago—only we couldn't find you to tell you so. You must come in as a friend and join my birthday party."

The man refused. He said, "No, I've worked all these years to pay you back. I can't think of myself as your friend until you have accepted my reparations. Otherwise, I'd feel like a hypocrite at your birthday party." He left and sat in the park across from the house and watched people going in to the festivities. He was angry, and his heart gnawed at him because his reparations had been refused and he felt he had been made light of.

As he sat there, the other man who had misused his employer's funds came past and went into the house. When he had entered, he made himself known and explained that he was there to repay the money he had lost all those years before. But when the employer recognized him, he exclaimed, "Oh, that's right! That's who you are. But I can't accept the money. I forgave the debt years ago—only we couldn't find you to tell you so. You must come in as a friend and join my birthday party."

The second man began to refuse like the first, saying, "No, I can't think of myself as your friend until you have accepted my reparations. Otherwise, I'll feel like a hypocrite…" But before he finished, he burst out laughing and said, "If you won't take this money back as reparation, then I give it to you as a birthday gift—and I accept your gracious invitation."

And the two of them went in to dinner.

L. William Countryman, *Forgiven and Forgiving* (Harrisburg, Pa.: Morehouse Publishing, 1998), 19–21.

Notes

INTRODUCTION

1. *The Life of Teresa of Jesus: The Autobiography of St. Teresa of Avila,* translated and edited by E. Allison Peers (New York: Image Books, 1960), 145.

2. See "Limits and Responsibilities of the *Companions in Christ: The Way of Forgiveness* Group" on page 16 in the Participant's Book.

3. W. Paul Jones, *A Season in the Desert: Making Time Holy* (Brewster, Mass.: Paraclete Press, 2000), 249–50.

WEEK 1: LIVING IN GOD'S BLESSING

1. Henri J. M. Nouwen, *The Return of the Prodigal Son: A Story of Homecoming* (New York: Image Books, 1994), 122.

2. Ibid.

WEEK 2: RELEASING SHAME AND GUILT

1. Charles Williams, *Descent into Hell* (Grand Rapids, Mich.: William B. Eerdmans Publishing Co., 1949), 99.

WEEK 3: FACING OUR ANGER

1. Henri J. M. Nouwen, *The Living Reminder: Service and Prayer in Memory of Jesus Christ* (New York: The Seabury Press, 1977), 23.

WEEK 6: FORGIVING OTHERS

1. Abbé de Tourville, *Letters of Direction: Thoughts on the Spiritual Life* (New York: Thomas Y. Crowell, 1959), 72.

About the Authors

Stephen D. Bryant is the World Editor and Publisher, Upper Room Ministries

Marjorie J. Thompson is the Director of the Pathways Center
for Spiritual Leadership, Upper Room Ministries

Evaluation

When your group has completed the *Companions in Christ: The Way of Forgiveness* resource, please share your insights and experiences in relation to the questions below. Use additional paper if needed.

1. Describe your group's experience with *Companions in Christ: The Way of Forgiveness*.

2. Did the resource lead your group to act in any concrete way as a reconciling community? If it did, please share your experience with us in this evaluation or through the discussion room at www.companionsinchrist.org.

3. How could *Companions in Christ: The Way of Forgiveness* be improved?

4. Do you have follow-up plans for your group? What resource do you plan to use, or what kinds of resources are you looking for?

Mail to: *Companions in Christ*
              Upper Room Ministries
              P. O. Box 340012
              Nashville, TN 37203-0012
Or fax: 615-340-7178

Prayers for Our COMPANIONS *in Christ*. Group
The Way of Forgiveness

We sign this card to indicate our desire to be *lifted in prayer* and to add our group's name to the listing on the website as we continue our *Companions in Christ* journey. This ministry of prayer for *Way of Forgiveness* groups is an offering of The Upper Room Living Prayer Center and its numerous covenant prayer groups across the country. These prayer groups have made a covenant to lift us as individuals and as a group in prayer once our card is received.

Leader Name: _____ Leader Email: _____

Church Name: _____

Church Address: _____

City/State/Zip: _____

Church Email: _____

All members are invited to sign their first name below.

Fold here and tape.

For information about dates and locations of *Companions in Christ* Leader Orientations (Basic One-Day Training) and Leader Trainings (Advance Three-Day Training) visit

www.companionsinchrist.org

Please include your return address:

_____

_____

_____

BUSINESS REPLY MAIL
FIRST-CLASS MAIL PERMIT NO. 1540 NASHVILLE TN

POSTAGE WILL BE PAID BY ADDRESSEE

COMPANIONS *in Christ*

UPPER ROOM MINISTRIES
PO BOX 340012
NASHVILLE, TN 37203-9540